KEITH LANE
WITH MARK HANKS

LIFE ON THE EDGE

THE TRUE STORY OF THE HERO
WHO SAVED THE LIVES OF TWENTY-NINE
PEOPLE AT BEACHY HEAD

JOHN BLAKE

Published by John Blake Publishing Ltd,
3 Bramber Court, 2 Bramber Road,
London W14 9PB, England

www.johnblakepublishing.co.uk

First published in paperback in 2010

ISBN: 978 1 84454 931 3

British Library Cataloguing-in-Publication Data:

A catalogue record for this book is available from the British Library.

Design by www.envydesign.co.uk

Printed in Great Britain by CPI Bookmarque, Croydon CR0 4TD

1 3 5 7 9 10 8 6 4 2

Papers used by John Blake Publishing are natural, recyclable products made from
wood grown in sustainable forests. The manufacturing processes conform to the
environmental regulations of the country of origin.

To Maggie

ACKNOWLEDGEMENTS

Enormous thanks to my wife, Val, who has supported me all the way, and to my two wonderful daughters, as well as the rest of my family. Special thanks to Ian Spratt, without whom the idea of doing a book would not have been born. Thanks also to Mark Hanks for all his help with writing the book and to John Blake Publishing for taking it on.

CONTENTS

FOREWORD

The doorbell rings and I jump up. I've been catnapping on and off for a few hours, but the sound of the bell jolts me back into reality. My wife is missing and the police are searching for her; I've been told to stay at home in case she returns. I walk towards the door, my head spinning. I guess it's the police and hope to God that it's good news.

Before I open up, I look out of the window. Two coppers. They're not the regular police, and their caps are in their hands. This is the moment it hits me. My wife is gone.

The world went suddenly strange. This isn't happening, I thought to myself, immediately in denial about the reality of the situation. I was like a goldfish in a bowl – everything around me was blurry, surreal, as if I was floating. I opened the door on autopilot, showed the policemen in and offered them tea as if nothing was amiss.

'It's all right, Mr Lane,' one of them said gently, 'I'll make us a cup of tea.'

But I wouldn't let them. I dashed into the kitchen and dizzily tried to pick up the kettle, prepare the cups and the milk, yet I was shaking like mad and could hardly get a grip on anything. I knew what news awaited me when I went back into the lounge and I wanted to delay the moment I heard it for as long as possible. It was as if the longer I put off the inevitable, the greater the chance it wasn't true.

But it was true. Horribly true. Sure enough, one of the policemen began to speak. I could only listen as he delivered the most devastating words a man could ever dream of hearing.

'I'm sorry, Mr Lane,' he said gently as he placed his arm on my shoulder, 'but I do believe we've found your wife, Maggie. I'm afraid she went over the cliff at Beachy Head. We found her in a crevice.'

My head shook from side to side. 'You don't know that,' I said, half-shouting, half-crying, 'you can't be sure it's her. How can you know?'

They told me they were 99 per cent certain. Then they asked me what my wife had been wearing when she left the house that morning. I knew, because I had laid her clothes out, ready for her to put on after she had showered. To this day I can still picture her black trousers and black-and-white top spread out on our bed.

'Well, this lady fits that description. She was wearing black and white,' the copper said softly. 'She is blonde and she's small and...'

There was no need for him to go on; his words confirmed what I'd been trying to deny. That was enough: I broke down. Words are not enough to describe that crushing feeling. I could hardly take it in. It wasn't like a punch to the stomach; it wasn't like having the ground taken from beneath my feet. It wasn't like anything on earth but... total devastation.

I'd lost the love of my life. I would never see her again. My precious, beloved Maggie was lying dead at the bottom of the cliff she had thrown herself from. In a couple of moments my entire world had collapsed. Nothing would ever be the same again and I didn't know what on earth to do.

Nothing could have prepared me for losing my wife. Maggie Lane was the love of my life, my soul mate, and now suddenly she was gone. Nobody could have told me what an extraordinary journey my time with her would lead me on. Nor could they have told me that one day I would write a book about it.

But before I begin to tell you about that journey, I must go back and tell you about Maggie. For without her, none of this would have happened.

CHAPTER 1

MAGGIE AND ME –
A LOVE STORY

I'll never forget the night I met the woman who was to become the love of my life – especially because, at that point, women were the last thing on my mind. It hadn't been long since I'd split up with my previous wife, although in the end it turned out to be a good thing that we'd gone our separate ways. Nevertheless, I was still smarting from the pain of it all. In fact, I had a bit of a downer on women at the time. All I was interested in was getting on with my life, without the complications of a relationship.

To take my mind off things, I'd started going out with one of my mates – a guy called Stevie – to play snooker every Thursday night and we'd always stop off at the pub for a few pints on the way home. I looked forward to it eagerly and we always had a good laugh together after our snooker games.

One Thursday, I was standing in the pub, pint in hand, chatting away with my mate when something pretty unremarkable happened – a petite blonde woman walked around the corner of the bar with a smile on her face. It's what happened next that was out of the ordinary. We locked eyes and – wham! – It was like something from a Mills & Boon story. It was love at first sight. I'd never experienced such an overwhelming feeling of attraction. This woman was like a vision and I could hardly believe she was really standing there. It was even harder to believe was that she was locking eyes with *me*. It was as if the rest of the room ceased to exist for those few moments. I could use every cliché in the book to describe how it felt to be staring into her eyes, but I won't. Safe to say, this woman was all I could see.

She was with a group of people in a pub quiz and by coincidence another friend of mine happened to be with them. I had a few words with him and he agreed to introduce us. Great, I thought, this is my chance. The problem was that when it came to saying hello to this stunning creature, I acted like a fumbling idiot. I was nervous and out of practice with women and I couldn't think of a thing to say. Not only was my tongue tied in a double knot, but my hands were flying in and out of my pockets as I shuffled from foot to foot. I felt like a right prat as I stumbled awkwardly through our conversation. Lord knows what we talked about, but soon enough it came to an abrupt end.

'Oh, I've got to go back to the quiz now,' she said, looking

2

over her shoulder towards her group of friends. 'By the way,' she added, 'my name is Maggie.'

'Oh, I'm sorry,' I replied hastily, 'I'm Keith.' *Damn*, I thought, I haven't even asked her name.

'Pleased to meet you…' she said as she wandered off into the other room.

I thought I'd totally blown it. Stevie came up and began digging me in the side, egging me on with a jokey 'Fill your boots! Fill your boots!', but he didn't realise how awkwardly I'd just acted. Suddenly I was no longer in the mood for a pint. Dejected and annoyed, I left soon afterwards and cursed myself all the way home. You idiot, I thought, you bloody idiot. You've seen someone you really like and you didn't even have the nerve to ask for her number. I was pretty down on myself about it and as I got into bed all I could think about was the likelihood that I would never see the lovely Maggie again.

A week passed. Before I knew it, Thursday had come around again and I was back down the snooker club. Stevie and I made our way to the pub after our game as usual, and I was hoping beyond hope that Maggie might be there. All I wanted was another chance – if I got it, I was going to make damn sure I didn't muck up this time around. And lo and behold, I got my chance.

I walked into the pub and there she was. Much later, Maggie admitted that she'd been desperately hoping that I would be there too – like me, she'd spent the week since our first encounter worried sick that she'd never see me again. She even confided that she didn't much like anyone from her quiz group and the only reason she'd come back a second time was the thought that I might show up again.

Things were different this time around. Fortune had smiled on me and given me a second crack at the whip, but I wasn't dumb enough to think I'd get a third. It was now or never and, thanks to my mate prodding me in the back, I got up the nerve to talk to her: I strode up, said hello and asked her what she was doing after the quiz.

'Nothing in particular,' she said, beaming.

'Well,' I went on, 'do you fancy joining us for a drink?'

Indeed she did. I was over the moon but still spent the time she was off at the quiz worrying about what I would say now I'd broken the ice. As I mentioned, I'd had my confidence shaken by my recent separation and was completely out of practice at this sort of thing! By the time Maggie sat down next to me with her drink, I was like a nervous teenager. I was talking about the most random stuff, everything and nothing. Although the conversation went fine, I was too nervous to really move on from polite small talk. I wanted to make an impression, but before I was able to try, Stevie did the job for me.

'Excuse me,' he said, leaning in to us, and looking at Maggie. 'My mate here thinks you're the bee's knees. He said he'd love to snog you, you know!'

I was instantly mortified, of course. I might not have been

doing a Casanova, but I sure didn't need my buddy to muscle in like we were a pair of schoolboys. However, I needn't have worried, for Maggie simply smiled and looked at me endearingly. That look told me all I needed to know. She liked me, she *wanted* to be talking to me and I didn't have to put on an act. In fact, her smile told me that she probably wanted to snog me too!

The three of us left the pub, and I dropped Stevie home before driving Maggie back to her flat. It was so wonderful being in the car with her: there was that immediate sense of calm and happiness that two people feel when they really get on — not to mention all the butterflies and nervous excitement that come when you begin to fall in love.

We arrived at Maggie's place and she invited me in for coffee...

Waking up in each other's arms was incredible. I was in love again. I knew it.

★   ★   ★

Both of us had just come out of long relationships. Both of us had been hurt in different ways and both of us were wary of getting involved in anything new. But our feelings for each other meant that it was hard to hold back for long. We got on too well and had too much of a good time to be worrying about the past.

Maggie was fun, bubbly, gorgeous — to me, the most gorgeous person I'd ever seen — and her lust for life and enthusiasm made me feel incredible. I hadn't felt quite alive for a while but Maggie was bringing out the best in me. People had noticed how miserable I'd been since splitting up with my wife, but now I was alive and kicking again and back to the old happy-go-lucky Keith that everyone used to know. People were shocked but delighted to see me telling jokes and being the life and soul of the party once more. It was great to be feeling myself again.

In the beginning we only saw each other twice a week, but on those nights we were inseparable. They say that 'love is blind' and we certainly lived up to the saying, going out on the town and carrying on like a couple of lovesick teenagers. The great thing was that Maggie didn't give a hoot about what anybody thought.

We were in our bubble and would do the daftest things. I'll never forget one night early on when we were out for a meal and Maggie politely asked me if I'd like a sip of her wine.

'Yes,' I replied graciously. 'Certainly I would!'

Little did I know precisely how she intended to supply that sip. Instead of passing me her glass, Maggie leaned across the table to kiss me… and poured a good half-glass worth of wine from her mouth into mine! Not the way two fortysomethings should carry on, perhaps, but we couldn't have cared less. It gave rise to another liberating moment of laughter and we were totally oblivious to the looks of the other diners around us.

We soon began to realise just how close we were becoming. We had the same outlook on life, the same love of adventure and fun and were falling deeply in love. Within a couple of months I was spending six out of seven nights with her. At first, Maggie reserved Thursday night for herself, for a spot of pampering, but she grew bored of being without me and soon I was there seven nights a week. That's what led to her moving in with me – it seemed ridiculous to have two homes when we only spent time in one.

There was something else ridiculous about the situation: I'd met the woman of my dreams, but I wasn't yet engaged to her! Within a couple of months of meeting her, I booked us flights to Paris and asked Maggie to marry me. We were at the top of the Eiffel Tower, it was pouring with torrential November rain, but even so I got down on one knee and proposed.

She said 'yes' and I felt like I was in heaven. On 21 May, 1999, only seven months after Maggie Lane had walked around the corner of the bar and locked eyes with me, I married her at Eastbourne Town Hall – and nothing could have made me happier.

* * *

The first couple of years of our marriage were bliss. We worked hard, played hard, went on holiday and did all the things that people in love should do. And still we carried on like a pair of 18-year-olds most of the time! Life was better

than I'd ever imagined it could be and I felt truly blessed.
Nobody could have persuaded me that such complete
happiness could soon start fall away, to be replaced by
something altogether darker and more destructive.

CHAPTER 2
CHANGES

I opened the cupboard under the sink. I'd been looking for my shoe polish and Maggie had told me that's where it was. I knelt there for a second and sure enough the shoe polish was staring me right in the face. But behind it, at the back of the cupboard, there was something else. Something I knew didn't belong under the sink. I reached in and picked it up.

It was a bottle of vodka.

A little confused, I didn't say anything for a few moments. We had a drinks cabinet and it had a bottle of vodka in it, so what was *this* bottle doing here? It was three-quarters empty, and I'd never seen it – let alone drunk from it – before, so it was pretty obvious that someone had been at it – and pretty obvious it was Maggie. I was cross. Why the need for secret drinking? I asked myself. I decided to approach Maggie about it calmly. Perhaps there was a rational explanation.

'What's this, sweetheart?' I asked, holding up the bottle.

'A bottle of vodka,' she replied.

'Yes, but what's it doing under the sink?' I enquired, gently.

'I don't know. I've never seen it before,' replied Maggie nonchalantly, as if to wave the whole subject away. Something about her manner told me she was lying and I felt myself getting angry.

'Are you drinking behind my back?'

'No,' she answered, flatly. I hardly knew what to say.

'Well, I don't drink vodka,' I replied. 'I'm not drinking it, so who is – mice? Are they having parties in here? Do we have a house of drunk mice?'

'No, no,' she said, lightly, 'it must have been a bottle I thought was empty and put in there to be thrown away.'

Maggie spoke as if it was a trivial matter, a mistake she had made, but I just couldn't buy her story.

'Come off it,' I said, a touch of exasperation in my voice, a hint of anger. 'Who are you kidding?'

'No one, Keith,' she protested, 'I'm not kidding anyone. I love you and I wouldn't do that to you, believe me.'

I didn't have much choice except to try and believe her. But I couldn't. Looking back, I suppose that moment marked the point I realised that all was not well with my beloved wife. Little did I know how bad things would get; little did I know how much trouble Maggie was already in.

From the moment we met, drinking had been part of our relationship. Social drinking, that is. Maggie and I were frequently out either with friends or each other, and more often than not we'd enjoy a good drink like anybody else. And on the weekends, we'd often get drunk and have fun together. It was all in the spirit of good fun; as far as I was concerned, alcohol was merely something that enhanced an already wonderful situation. I'm sure we would have had just as much love and fun without it, but I never questioned whether or not drinking was a problem because, for me at least, it wasn't.

The discovery that Maggie was drinking behind my back made me question things. Why did she feel the need to hide it from me? I asked myself. How much was she drinking? And more to the point, *what was driving her to it?*

When I thought about it, I felt sure I knew part of the answer. Two things had happened in recent months that Maggie hadn't taken well. Firstly, she'd started going through the menopause. The hormonal changes had affected her moods and were making her feel slightly down. Secondly, Maggie had recently lost a job. The job was great and so were most of the people she had worked with, but eventually it came to a point where she faced the choice of resigning or getting the sack. To cut a long story short, a situation had arisen where it had looked as if Maggie has mucked up when, in fact, she hadn't. It was terrible for me to witness my beloved being made unhappy and losing the job really affected her.

Both of these events led to a noticeable change in Maggie. Before, everything had been so much fun – Maggie was always her bubbly self and we were enjoying life to the full – whereas now the woman I knew was gone. Instead of a smiling face at the end of a day, I would come home to find a long one. The Maggie who had always loved getting out, having adventures, socialising and filling a room with laughter had been replaced by someone who would opt for sitting at home on the couch. We'd always had a passionate sex life, but now that went out of the window too.

All of these things were bad, and it was obvious Maggie was having a rough time, but I thought it was merely a phase – nothing a bit of TLC and encouragement couldn't remedy. I'd go out of my way to buy her flowers, surprise her with ideas, give her massages, talk to her and try to help her think her way out of her worries, but it all seemed in vain.

Maggie's problems were significant – I understood that – but were they bad enough to lead her to drink in secret? Certainly she had not been herself, but until I found that vodka I hadn't realised the extent to which she must have been feeling unhappy. Hearing her lie to me about it made me realise that she must be in a pretty bad place. After all, I knew she loved me and for someone to lie in that way means they've become pretty messed-up inside.

It didn't take long before I realised Maggie wasn't simply unhappy: she was suffering with depression and was drinking in order to try and get herself through it. The worst part is that the booze would have been making her worse – after all, alcohol is itself a depressant, so she was already in a vicious cycle. A fundamental aspect of depression is that the sufferer ceases to look at the world in a rational way. Little things get blown out of all proportion and a depressed person has no way of talking themselves out of feeling bad. Depression is an illness and often responds well to treatment, but it's making sure people receive the treatment that's important.

If I'd known then what I know now about depression, I would have done some things differently. I would have tried to get Maggie professional help straight away. She had been to the doctor and was already taking antidepressants; I assumed that, in addition to the pills, my help would be enough to get her back to normal.

It's a helpless feeling watching a loved one go through any sort of pain, and I could see Maggie was enduring a lot of mental anguish. In response, I did what I thought was the best thing: in the period following the vodka incident, I thought that I would try and catch Maggie out again in order to get her to 'own up' to what was going on. If this happened, I reasoned, the confrontation would encourage her to stop her behaviour, or agree to seek help for it.

Maggie would often wake in the night and go downstairs for a glass of water or juice, and I'd never questioned it before – I simply wished she were a better sleeper. But now I knew about the secret drinking, I began to wonder if her trips downstairs were for alcohol. I had to find out if my suspicions were justified, so one night I crept downstairs after her. I felt like a right bastard to be doing such a thing, and to this day I still hate myself for it. After all, it's a sad state of affairs if a man is sneaking up on his wife, especially if he loves her in the way that I loved Maggie. It broke my heart that I'd got to the point where I didn't trust her as much as before, but I was desperate to find out the truth.

The house was silent. I tiptoed through the lounge towards the kitchen. The door between the two was open, and once I got to within a few feet of it, I froze. There was my wife, standing in the half-light, drinking vodka in the middle of the night. The real shock was the way she was drinking it – she had her head tilted back and was swigging it straight from the bottle. It was a heartbreaking sight, and confirmed my worst fears. A few moments passed as I stood there, mouth agape, in stunned silence.

Maggie became aware of my presence, for suddenly she stopped drinking and shot a guilty glance at me. 'What?' she said.

'What are you doing?' I asked incredulously, trying to remain calm and measured.

'Nothing, sweetheart, I was just checking to see how much was in there.'

Such a bare-faced lie made me angry, yet sad at the same time. However bad it was for me to be witnessing this, Maggie's state of mind must have been a hundred times worse – denial on that scale is a scary thing. I tried to talk reasonably.

'You were drinking it, sweetheart,' I said calmly. 'It's OK, but you were drinking it. I know you were.'

But it was no good. Maggie wouldn't accept what I was saying and a huge argument erupted. It was the first major row of our relationship.

'How *dare* you creep up on me,' Maggie shouted, 'You've no right to do that. I'm an individual and you're invading my privacy!'

'Yeah, well I'm an individual too and I've got a right to know what damage my wife is doing to herself!' I retorted. 'I've never tried to stop you drinking. We keep our drinks in the cabinet, so why the need to drink behind my back?'

We yelled back and forth at each other. It was ugly. I was on the offensive, offloading all the pain and confusion I had about Maggie's behaviour, and she was on the defensive, telling me it was none of my business. We shouted ourselves out until, suddenly, we threw ourselves into each other's arms and both broke down in tears. I cried because we'd been arguing, because I didn't understand how things had come to this, because it was so terrible to see my Maggie in such a state – I still call her 'my Maggie' to this day – and because I was so desperate to help. I'm sure Maggie's tears flowed for similar reasons and I'm sure she was also crying because she knew she was so lost and depressed, because she couldn't see a way out.

Strangely, afterwards we ended up making passionate love together for the first time in quite a while. Despite the painfulness of our argument, fighting had brought us closer than we'd been in weeks. We both loved each other, after all, and for a few moments the distance that Maggie's depression had put between us seemed smaller.

We lay in bed together afterwards, holding each other close. The shouting was over. Finally we were talking openly again.

CHAPTER 3

ROAD TO RECOVERY, ROAD TO RUIN

With depression and alcoholism, a person must recognise and accept they have a problem before they can begin to deal with it. The same goes for any illness, of course. Recognition is the first big step to recovery. Maggie was suffering from both depression and dependency on alcohol and as we lay in bed in the early hours, I brought the subject up with her.

'Sweetheart,' I began, 'I love you more than anything and that's why I'm going to say what I'm about to say. I think you have a problem with alcohol. I think you need help. You need to see someone about your drinking – a counsellor, perhaps.'

Maggie nodded. She seemed to agree. For the first time I was getting through to her and I felt a massive sense of relief.

Maggie agreed to go to Alcoholics Anonymous and I was quietly over the moon.

The meetings helped her; I encouraged her and Maggie went teetotal. It was amazing how quickly things began to get back to normal. It was as if the real Maggie had finally returned from a long holiday, and as each day went by I could see her improving. The difference was incredible and obvious. Just as my family had thanked Maggie for coming into my life and bringing me back to my old self, Maggie's family thanked me for encouraging her to lay off the booze. They cared for her deeply and had been as worried as I was about her downward spiral. We were all so happy to see her nearly back once more to being the bubbly woman we loved. She was still on anti-depressants, but now she was off the drink they were working properly – it's well known that alcohol will interfere with (and render useless) most psychoactive drugs.

To my delight, she decided she was ready to go back to work, so began temping locally while she looked for a full-time job. It was wonderful to see her flinging herself at life again instead of sitting at home. But there was a problem. For one reason or another, things kept going wrong at work. A job would end, and she'd have difficulty finding another. Eventually she'd find one but then get knocked back again after a few weeks. With the memory of the job she had loved in her mind, Maggie found it hard to find anything to match it and this started to get her down. After several kicks in the teeth, her moods began to dip again. She hadn't had a drink for three months, but towards the end of that period she must have started to lose faith again. And that's when she turned back to the bottle.

When Maggie agreed to stop drinking, I felt she'd taken the first big step to becoming well again. Indeed by stopping drinking she had taken a huge step. But what I didn't consider at the time was exactly why. Looking back, I can see that she was doing it for me, because she loved me, because she could see the damage that it was doing to our relationship. And that's the point – she was doing it for me, but not for herself. Maggie was still in the grip of alcohol even when she wasn't drinking. Even though she was sober, she still wanted to be drinking. Giving up required strength – and boy, she could be strong when she wanted to – but when a person has deep-rooted problems, those problems often win out. Maggie's resolve went because her problems overwhelmed her again.

I began to find booze hidden away again and it was a real blow. I felt we'd come so far. It wasn't that I was sad for myself. I was sad for my wife and I didn't know what to do. This time around, Maggie's drinking was worse than before. It became more secretive and now I'd even find small bottles tucked away at the bottom of her handbag. Maggie began to drink throughout the day and would even fill up water bottles with vodka so that she could drink in public and at work without raising any eyebrows. It was such a sad time, and there was very little I could do to stop her. It was as if she'd resigned herself to being a drinker. Before long she was physically dependent on alcohol and would drink any time, morning noon and night. If Maggie didn't have access to liquor she would be in a real state – mentally agitated and physically shaky – yet even though it was obvious how dependent she was, she would still frequently deny that she was drinking.

I remember coming home from golf one day and finding what looked like a glass of orange juice on the bedside table. I picked it up and could smell vodka in it. When I asked her about it she was adamant that it was just orange. There was no point in getting into an argument, so I left it. Watching a person in denial is a frustrating thing and I used to boil up inside whenever Maggie lied in such a way, but I would always try and count to ten and walk away – labouring the point would have been destructive and a waste of time. When someone is so deeply in denial they have got to a point where they really believe what they are saying. It's hard to comprehend, but this is what happened to Maggie.

On occasions, it was really hard to control my anger and frustration. There were a number of times when Maggie would lock herself in the bathroom for no reason other than to be able to drink. I'd be around the house and eventually realise where she was before walking up the stairs to try and coax her out gently. But most of the time talking was no use – Maggie either didn't want to come out or she was too drunk to respond to me coherently. In the end, I'd have to resort to threatening to kick the door down – sometimes I even began to kick it pretty hard, though I never actually kicked it in – and it was only then that she would open up, fall into my arms and cry. I'd try and be positive, telling her that we could get through this, that things could be OK again, but things only went from bad to worse.

I'd find Maggie really out of it, being sick down the toilet and over herself, and the process of cleaning everything up and trying to straighten her out broke my heart. All the time this was going on I would think back to the woman I once knew and wonder how things had got so bad. I sometimes asked myself whether it was all my fault. Looking back, I think I can say it wasn't, for I would soon discover that there were more contributing factors to Maggie's depression than her life as it stood – she had a dark past – and I would soon be given a glimpse into it. But something truly awful was to happen first.

My wife would try to kill herself.

I came home from a busy day at work. Maggie was nowhere to be seen downstairs – as was often the case these days – so I walked upstairs to find her. My first reaction to what I found was complete shock. For a few moments I simply froze. Maggie was in the bedroom, sprawled on the bed, passed out with her head tilted back and her eyes rolled back, an empty bottle by her side, along with an empty packet of antidepressants. The realisation that she had

21

overdosed hit me and after a couple of seconds I leaped into action, rushed down the stairs and dialled 999. The voice at the end of the line told me to leave the front door open, go back upstairs and try to wake Maggie up. Once back at her side I shook her, kissed her and did everything I could to try and bring her back to consciousness. Maggie came round a tiny bit and began murmuring, but it was hard to keep her awake – her eyes were rolling and her body was completely limp. All I could do was hold her and call her name in an effort to keep her with me.

I can barely describe the feeling of being on that bed by Maggie's side. When I first found her, the adrenaline kicked in and I simply went into a practical mode. But I had time to think once I had called the ambulance and managed to bring her round a little. And that's when the fear kicked in. The reality of the situation hit me like a hammer and I began to tremble and sweat with sheer panic. The woman I loved so dearly was lying in my arms and close to death yet there was nothing I could do but wait. I felt so lonely and useless, paralysed with terror that my Maggie was about to die.

'Don't worry, she's going to be OK,' the paramedics reassured me after several minutes of working on her. Those words were like a ten tonne weight being lifted from my shoulders. They strapped an oxygen mask to her face, and whisked her off to A & E. I followed in the car, and after hours of vomiting and rest Maggie eventually came round fully.

A psychiatrist assessed her, told me that Maggie needed help and arranged for her to see a counsellor once a week. Maggie agreed to the arrangement, but she was more concerned with the fact that she'd put me through the mill again. She was full of apologies and I know she really was sorry. To an outsider, it may appear as if Maggie's behaviour was purely selfish, but I don't see it that way at all. I saw that what she was going through was part of an illness. Sure, that illness meant I had to go through a lot of shit with her, but I went through it because I loved her so much and believed we could get through it.

It used to make me really mad when people said how awful it was that Maggie was putting me through so much. 'Don't you dare judge Maggie, nor me,' I'd reply. 'If you had cancer and were being sick all over the place, would you like to have your better half look after you? Of course you would, so don't slam her or me just because her illness has a stigma attached to it.'

I don't care how much Maggie made my life difficult – I won't hear a bad word said about her. I chose to stay with her because I loved her and that's it. It wasn't me that was a victim, it was her. Seeing her in that hospital made it very obvious who was suffering the most and when she said sorry and that she would try to get better I could tell that she meant it. Yet, looking back, I can see that she was so trapped in her illness that she only wanted to get better for my sake. Once again it was me that was putting the words in her mouth.

I asked her if there was anything I could do to help her and she told me that I couldn't do anything more than I was already doing. I remember telling her that she needed to give up not for me, but for her. She would nod in response and say 'Of course I'll stop', but not once did she say that she needed to give up for her sake, for *our* sake. I think the points at which Maggie said she would stop are comparable to the situation of a husband who beats his wife but insists he will stop – at the time he says it, when all the remorse and regret is there, he truly believes that he won't hit her again. Time passes, however, and the original unresolved problem overwhelms the man, whatever his good intentions, and he does it again.

We left the hospital and the cycle started all over again. For a while Maggie stopped, but then she lapsed once more. This went on and on, and every time she lapsed she fell further and crashed harder than before. She began to disappear from the house and stay out for hours and hours without letting me know where she was. Because of her history with booze, I found this hard to bear. The worry her disappearances caused me was overwhelming. On countless occasions I'd let the clock tick until I could bear it no longer – your imagination goes wild when someone you love goes missing, especially when they have a problem. I used to worry that she was in a bar somewhere, smashed out of her head, and that someone might take advantage of her – rape her, murder her even. The paranoia would set in and a number of times I had to call the police to help me find her.

I remember one night when I'd been waiting for Maggie for hours and hours. Eventually, at around 11.30 pm, she called. Her speech was so slurred that I could barely understand what she was saying, but I managed to glean that she had booked herself into a hotel. I drove over and picked her up – literally – before driving home. When we pulled up outside the house, I opened the car door and went to support her. But I misjudged it a little and she collapsed in a heap on the kerb.

As I carried her towards the house I could see a few of the neighbours' curtains twitching and I knew we were being watched. It sounds awful, but when you have the one you love in your arms, and she's completely drunk again, and people are watching, it is embarrassing. I felt bad for Maggie's indignity, and I felt bad for myself – I suppose it was only natural. I propped Maggie up against the wall while I opened the door, then carried her inside. I struggled up the stairs, undressed her and put her into bed.

Then I wept.

It was one of the first times I'd really cried about it all. I'd been holding so much in and had been hoping that things would work out for so long, but that night I just began to fall apart a little. I sat on the edge of the bed, stroking Maggie's head and crying my eyes out. I couldn't believe this was happening. I didn't know which way to turn any more. I'm doing all I can here, I thought to myself. I've got her counselling, I've got her to AA and I'm giving her all the support I can, so why is she not responding? What am I doing so wrong, for God's sake?

I knew that there would be the usual apology in the morning. There was, but with a heartbreaking twist.

'I've really hurt you this time, haven't I?' said Maggie, her face filled with remorse and sadness.

'Yes,' I said. I couldn't lie to her. The situation was tearing me up inside.

'Well, OK, go on then,' she said meekly. I had no idea what she was talking about.

'What do you mean, "Go on then"?' I replied, confused.

'Go on,' she replied, 'hit me.'

I was dumbstruck. 'Why would I hit you?' I said incredulously. I could hardly believe the words had come from my wife's mouth.

'Because that's what men do. It's what I deserve. I've always been hit. I've always been beaten.'

To realise that Maggie felt this way about herself, to know that she thought I wanted to hit her, broke my heart. I took her hands in mine and looked right into her eyes.

'I would never touch a hair on your head apart from to care for you,' I told her firmly.

'Hit me,' she said again, 'just give me a good hiding and it will all be forgotten.'

'No,' I protested, 'I won't hit you, and I'll never hit you as long as I live. If I ever went for you it would be over. I'd walk because we'd be finished.'

'Well, what can I do to make it up to you?' she asked.

'All you can do for me is get better, darling,' I said as tears began to stream from my eyes. 'I love you so deeply that it's all I want.'

It was one of the most depressing conversations I've ever had, but it offered me a little more insight into the causes of Maggie's depression. In the past, long before we met, she had taken several beatings. I began to think that it was her past that was haunting her and I wondered if addressing whatever demons lurked there might help her.

It was when Maggie attempted to slit her wrists that I decided to try and get to the bottom of her past, and that's because I saw this incident as little more than a cry for help – I didn't believe that Maggie really wanted to die, but I felt she was calling out for someone to rescue her. The attempt itself was almost half-hearted, if that doesn't sound too unsympathetic. Rather than a knife, Maggie used a razor blade and didn't take the cover off. Perhaps it was because she was too drunk – who knows? – but she only had a few scratches down her arms. I took her cry for help as an opportunity to play the psychiatrist and try to understand her past in order to hopefully help the present. Maybe, I thought, just maybe, if Maggie can exorcize her demons with me, if she can face up to whatever is haunting her, then she'll be happy in herself, get her confidence back and be able to face the problem of the demon drink. Perhaps it was wishful thinking, but I was desperate to explore any avenue that might lead to Maggie getting well.

So I started to ask about her past and, indeed, she'd had her fair share of trouble. She told me that her problems had started from an early age. Her mother died when Maggie was only three and her father destroyed all the photos of her, so Maggie never got to find out what she looked like. Her dad found someone else, who became Maggie's stepmum, and there was a lot of friction between Maggie and her. Put simply, Maggie received some pretty awful treatment at her stepmum's hands – she told me that she was locked in cupboards as a punishment for minor things, that she was beaten regularly and that she had vivid memories of lying on the floor, crying, and her stepmother simply walking over her. To make matters worse, her stepmother would tell her father that Maggie had been bad when she hadn't, which resulted in Maggie being banished to her room – punished for no good reason. This was very painful for her, because until her stepmum came along Maggie had received a huge amount of love and affection from her father. She had fond memories of sitting on his lap listening to nursery rhymes, and of feeling warm and secure when he read bedtime stories to her. Yet once Maggie's stepmum arrived on the scene and began telling fibs about her, the affection dropped away and he began to lock her in her room. In Maggie's mind, within a year of losing her mum she had lost her dad too.

Anyone with negative early experiences is likely to have problems with self-esteem and depression as they get older. To feel rejected by your own family sets you up for a life of feeling bad about yourself, of feeling you don't deserve affection, and makes you far more likely to get into bad relationships where it is somehow 'the norm' to be treated badly. I think Maggie's past partly explains why she ended up going for men who treated her unkindly – it was a weird way of replicating what she know best and of letting history repeat itself. When you're a kid and the version of 'affection' you get is mucked up, you're going to take that on with you in life.

Some people can deal with the problems they faced in childhood – whether it be through therapy, talking to friends, or just thinking long and hard – but I don't think Maggie ever came to terms with the traumas of her past. What's more, I know I never got her whole story from her – I can never shake from my mind something she said to me a number of times when we talked about her past. 'You'll never know the whole truth,' she'd say through her tears with deadly seriousness, but no matter how much I probed she would not elaborate on certain areas. Quite obviously, things had happened to Maggie that were just too painful for her to talk about.

I know there are two sides to every story and I was always conscious of this when listening to Maggie's point of view about her past. It's often natural for a person to exaggerate and sometimes I asked myself whether or not she was bending the truth in some way. My gut feeling is that she wasn't because I could see so clearly how depressed she was and how much her past haunted her. I may be wrong, but I don't think Maggie would have ended up with such bad depression, or such an addictive personality, were it not for her troubled past.

Talking about her history may have helped Maggie get things off her chest, and it gave me more insight into what lay behind her drinking and depression, but it didn't help with the problems of the present. Maggie's periods of sobriety shortened to the point that I was never sure if she was actually off the booze. I'd find it in any number of places around the house – at the back of cupboards, hidden in the linings of cushions and pillows – and Maggie knew I was looking too. 'Here comes old supersleuth,' she would joke sarcastically. 'Where are you going to look tonight, then?'

Trying to catch Maggie out all the time was probably not helpful, and it certainly didn't stop her from drinking, but I was in a position where I really didn't know what else to do. I'd tried everything to get her to stop, so at the very least I wanted to know what was going on and whether she was drinking or not. More often than not, she was.

Gradually, Maggie's disappearances became more frequent and she began to go missing overnight; it was agony not knowing where my wife was. She also took another couple of antidepressant overdoses, one of which caused her to have a fit that frightened the life out of me. I was at my wits' end, but I never thought about giving up hope.

During one spell in hospital, a psychiatrist asked Maggie if she realised how much her behaviour was damaging not just her, but me too. To this day I'm convinced that she took this on board and I think part of the reason Maggie ended up taking her life was that she didn't want to put me through such misery any more. She felt she would never get better and she didn't want to drag me along with her any longer.

Life was becoming very hard, and one day there came a moment where I thought the unthinkable; even now I'm ashamed to admit to a feeling that flashed through my mind one night. I had just returned home from a party. I'd had my doubts about going, because by that stage I didn't want to leave Maggie alone, but she had persuaded me that that she would be OK – all she wanted to do was sleep, she said. She wanted me to go and enjoy my evening. I went to the party, but I was so worried about what she might do in my absence that I only stayed for an hour before returning home. It turned out that I was right to be worried.

I found Maggie had overdosed again – the bottle and the empty sachet of pills were by the bed and on the bed itself was Maggie. She was absolutely out of it. Oh God, I thought, I can't take this any more, and for a brief moment I thought how it would be the easiest thing in the world to simply turn on my heel, walk out of the house and make out that I hadn't come home at all.

That's right: I thought about leaving my wife to die.

Needless to say, I didn't turn on my heel, and I hated myself for having even thought such a thing. But think it I did. Getting to the point where I could contemplate such a terrible thing made me realise just what an impossible situation Maggie and I were trapped in. Life had turned from a dream into a nightmare. Maggie was lost and so was I.

CHAPTER 4

GONE

It was 2 March 2004. A beautiful day. The sun shone brightly in a clear blue sky. The air was crisp and cold. I was on a window-cleaning job, feeling almost positive for a change – Maggie had set off from the house in the morning for a new temping job at a company called Marlow Ropes. Although I had the usual worries and fears about her, and the familiar butterflies in my stomach as I wondered how her day would go, the weather was lifting my spirits.

Before we had parted, I'd wished Maggie good luck and kissed her on the cheek. 'Goodbye, darling,' I said, 'I love you.'

'Love you too,' she replied as always.

My mobile rang around lunchtime. It was Maggie.

'Hello sweetheart,' I said, 'how's the job going?'

'Oh, not my cup of tea,' she replied, 'though I need

the money. I'm going to have lunch and then I'm going to go back.'

There was nothing odd in what Maggie said, but her tone of voice was strange. She sounded slightly slurred and I could tell something was not quite right. Here we go again, I thought, and prepared myself for another difficult episode. At the same time, I wondered if there was anything I could do to nip it in the bud.

'Sweetheart,' I said, 'would you like me to come over? You don't sound quite right.'

Maggie insisted she was fine. I persisted for a bit, offering to come and meet her for lunch. But she was adamant that all was well.

'I'm fine,' she repeated. 'I'm going back to work in a minute. What I want you to do is put some jacket potatoes in the oven when you get home tonight. I'll get the chilli ready when I get back.'

Her words were enough to reassure me. After all, if she was planning dinner in such a casual, normal way, perhaps everything was OK. Maybe I was just being over-anxious.

'OK, darling,' I replied, 'I'll see you later. Love you.'

'I love you, sweetheart,' she answered, and hung up.

Little did I know those were the last words Maggie would ever speak to me.

Once we'd hung up I became anxious again. I spoke to a friend and told her I wasn't happy. 'Don't worry,' she said. 'Maggie'll be OK.' So I went back to work.

Later, on my way home, I stopped off to buy a CD. At Christmas, my daughter had played an album by Evanescence and Maggie had loved it. I bought it thinking she would love the surprise when she got home. I was always trying to do things that would make her happy and perhaps reduce her need to drink.

I got home, put the potatoes on and placed the CD in the player. I was ready. There was nothing left to do but wait for Maggie to come home, so I sat down. I was excited at the thought of her walking in the door and being surprised by my little treat.

I waited for an hour, but there was no sign of her. The jackets were well on the way to being cooked, so I turned the oven down. I called her mobile but it rang out. Oh God, I thought with a familiar sense of dread, she's gone off on one of her jaunts again. All the usual worries flooded my mind. Which pub is she in? Is she going to go to a hotel again? Am I going to get a phone call later?

Another hour went by. The jacket potatoes were more than done by now, so I turned the oven off. What a waste of time. I tried her phone again. Nothing. Butterflies filled my stomach, and I started to feel sick. It was obvious Maggie was drinking somewhere. All I could do was call her again and again in case she had passed out – I hoped the phone might eventually wake her. But there was no answer.

I turned the events of the day over in my head. Already I was kicking myself for not having come home to check on her at lunch. Why didn't I go with my instincts? I thought. I'd been right – there must have been something wrong.

It was getting late. By 10 o'clock I was starting wonder what on earth to do – Should I go out looking for her? I wondered, but before I had a chance to take action, the doorbell rang.

For a second I thought it might be Maggie. It wasn't. It was the police.

'We saw your car on a patrol earlier today,' they told me, 'and it hasn't moved since then.'

Well, I thought, if she's been out drinking, then it would make sense that the car hasn't moved.

'So where's the car?' I asked them.

'Beachy Head.'

'No!' I shot back, incredulously.

'Yes, it's up there,' said one of the officers, 'but don't panic yet. We'll find her.'

Although Beachy Head is a well-known suicide hotspot, at first I didn't twig that the police were considering that she might be dead – I'm not sure why, but I just didn't. Also, I'd always seen Maggie's extreme acts, terrible though they were, as cries for help. She had always put herself in situations where she would be found alive. I simply didn't think she was prepared to kill herself.

Then, the police informed me that they'd sent a helicopter up to search for her – and it was at that moment that I began to really worry. I knew that those helicopters cost £2,500 an hour to run and they don't send them up unless there is real concern. They're equipped with a heat-seeking device for finding people who are alive – or recently dead.

The police told me to remain at home in case Maggie returned or called the landline. I gave them the spare keys to her car and off they went. As I watched them get into the patrol car and drive off towards Beachy Head, my heart filled with dread. This was new territory. Maggie wasn't in the pub. She wasn't in a hotel. She wasn't wandering the streets. She was at Beachy Head and had abandoned her car. By now I was absolutely shitting myself. Out of my mind with panic, I didn't know what to do. I paced up and down the house and began to shake like a leaf. I've never shaken like that and I didn't stop for two hours. Then, around 12.30 am, I looked out of the window and saw Maggie's car coming down the road.

Yes! I thought. They've found her and brought her back! Thank God.

I raced to the door, but Maggie was nowhere to be seen. All I could see were two police officers coming down the drive. As they came closer I could see that they had her handbag and her scarf with them. I waited for what they had to say with my heart in my mouth.

'The car is damaged but driveable,' one of them began. 'Maggie must have hit something. We're afraid there's no sign of her yet. The heat-seeking helicopter can't find anything up there.'

This offered me my first glimmer of hope – it was good

news that she was nowhere to be seen around Beachy Head. Typical Maggie, I thought with a degree of relief. She's buggered off again – probably to a hotel in town. But why, I thought, did she leave her handbag behind? And why hasn't she called? Perhaps she was too out of it to think straight.

The officers informed me that the search would begin again in the morning. For the moment there was nothing else they could do. They told me to get some sleep. Yeah, right! I thought to myself.

I didn't sleep a wink. I sat on the edge of the sofa all night, turning all the possibilities of what may have become of Maggie over and over in my head. As soon as first light broke, I jumped into my car and set off for Beachy Head.

Once there, I searched under bushes and behind trees – anywhere Maggie might have passed out. I didn't look over the cliff edge at first, but after I'd tried everywhere else I began peering over. I covered almost all of the three-mile stretch of cliff edge.

Nothing.

There was nowhere else to look, so I decided to begin searching the local hotels. I called my daughter and she joined me. I went to the Hydro Hotel first and asked the receptionist if they had a Mrs Lane staying with them.

'Yes, we do,' came the reply.

Pure relief coursed through my veins. We'd got her! My precious Maggie was safe.

'How old is Mrs Lane?' asked the receptionist.

'Fifty-four,' I replied. 'Why?'

'The Mrs Lane we have here is 88,' the receptionist replied.

That brought me crashing back down to earth. There was nothing for it but to carry on searching the other hotels. We searched for three more hours, but to no avail. I was knackered – I hadn't slept for 36 hours – so I went home and lay on the sofa.

The next thing I knew I was being jolted awake by the doorbell.

And that's when I found out that my wife was dead.

I couldn't take any of it in, I just couldn't. The rest of that day passed in a nightmarish blur. I can remember only fragments of it. I recall people – mostly family members – being in the lounge, and the atmosphere being one of total devastation. Everybody was crying hysterically, hugging and wailing. People wanted to hug me but I didn't want to be hugged. I didn't want anything but for this not to be happening. I felt like I was underwater – sounds and faces were a blur and I could barely register what was being said to me. People were trying to be supportive by trotting out lines such as 'Everything's going to be all right', but when I heard that I thought to myself, What the fuck are they talking about? They don't know what the fuck they're talking about. *Nothing's* going to be all right, *nothing*, so stick your stupid comments up your arse! I knew people meant well, but I just wanted them all to leave – leave, for God's sake! Eventually, they did.

At one point, a policeman broached the subject of identifying Maggie. 'I'm afraid you'll have to do it tomorrow,' he said. 'Unless someone else is able to do it for...' he continued as he looked around the room. But I cut him short.

'Nobody identifies my wife other than me,' I said loudly, with utter conviction. I don't remember much after that, apart from my younger daughter arriving. She came in and didn't say a word. She simply took me in her arms and held me, which is all you can do for someone in such a grief-stricken, shocking situation. There are no words of comfort that can help in such times and acknowledging this in the way that my daughter did is the best thing a loved one can do. We just hugged and hugged. After everyone else had left we just sat there talking and crying, trying to begin to come to terms with what had happened – and not even getting close. Eventually my mind and body gave way and I nodded off to sleep.

The next thing I knew, my daughter was waking me.

'Come on Dad,' she said softly. 'You've got to get washed and shaved. You've got to go and identify your Maggie.'

★　　　★　　　★

'Are you all right, Mr Lane?' asked the coroner as she approached me in the hospital foyer. Now, I realise that people have to go through the pleasantries, but I remember thinking what a bloody stupid question that was. I was anything but all right.

'I'll tell you what we're going to do,' she continued. 'We're going to walk to the mortuary, you'll be asked to enter and in order to confirm your wife's identity you must say the words, "That is my wife."'

'OK,' I replied, as I rose to my feet shakily. I was about to do something I'd never even dreamed I would have to do. But now it had to be done.

I was so weak that I could hardly walk – my brother took me on one side and my daughter got hold of the other so that we could follow the coroner down the long hospital corridor. I remember a blur of people, but it was as if they were from another world and I was just a silent witness to what was going on. Perhaps they felt the same about me. Tears streaked down my face as my loved ones propped me up, and I knew that every person we passed was looking at me. It was as if I was an animal in a zoo.

All those gawping people made me want to strike out, to say, 'What do you think you're looking at?' The moments of anger that hit you when you're grieving come out of nowhere and are sometimes hard to suppress. But I didn't strike out, I didn't say a word, I just kept on walking. Then, all of a sudden we were at the mortuary waiting room. This was it.

'Before you go in,' said the coroner, 'I must ask if you would like Maggie's clothes?'

I said I would like them and was handed two brown bags. One contained her clothes, the other her jewellery, including her engagement ring and her wedding ring. They were her things, but still I had to officially identify her.

I was shown the entrance to the room where her body lay. Slowly I walked toward the curtains that were draped across the door. I swept them aside and walked into the room. Once inside, I looked up. The image I was met with will never leave me.

It was Maggie.

Her head was the only part of her that was exposed. The rest of her body was covered by a blanket. I was staring at the woman who, only yesterday morning, had kissed me goodbye before work. Now she was dead on a slab.

I collapsed, slumping towards the floor. My brother and daughter caught me, took me from the room and sat me down. I hadn't said the words I needed to say. I still hadn't identified her.

'Are you ready to go back in again, Mr Lane?' enquired the coroner gently.

I nodded. I was ready.

I walked back in stood at the edge of the room. I looked up and began to cry.

'Yes, that's my Maggie,' I said, looking at her. Somehow, I couldn't leave the room right away. I needed some time. 'Could I have ten minutes on my own?' I asked.

'Of course you can,' came the reply.

Slowly I walked towards her. Once I got close I could see that this wasn't the Maggie I recognised. She was horribly battered and bruised. There was a gash across her left eyebrow, and a larger one down her side. The situation hardly felt real.

I put my hand under the blanket and took her hand. It was stone cold.

I stood there for ten minutes and cried my eyes out. I've never felt such a sense of confusion, such an overwhelming feeling of despair. As I cried, I spoke to Maggie's body through my tears.

'Why?' I said, 'Why did you do it? Why have you left me like this? You know how much I love you, you know how much I care for you, so why, why, *why*?'

Those moments of grief were a sort of hysteria and within that hysteria there were some selfish moments. 'How am I going to cope without you,' I said, half-shouting, half-crazed. 'What am I going to do?' They were awful things to say – my wife was dead and I was asking her how I was going to cope. At least I was alive!

Eventually I let go of Maggie's hand and walked out – in pieces. My daughter and brother held me for quite a while and we did nothing but cry. But it couldn't go on forever. Eventually, I picked up Maggie's belongings, walked back down the corridor, out of the hospital and back to the car.

I put my seatbelt on and then let out a huge sigh. It felt like it came from somewhere deep within me. I'm not sure quite what it was – exhaustion from the last 48 nearly sleepless hours of worry, or maybe a strange sense of relief.

All I knew was that I'd just spent my last moments with Maggie, and that it was time to go home.

Everyone experiences pain when they lose loved ones. Some people experience greater losses than I did – they lose their entire family in one go, they lose their children to war – and my experience was by no means unique or exceptional in the grand scheme of things. But it was special to me. Identifying my wife in that mortuary was the hardest thing I've ever had to do.

As I sat in the car in that car park, it was almost impossible to believe that the only thing to do next was to drive back to the home that we had once shared.

*   *   *

The next few days passed in an unreal haze. There were things to be done, people to contact and legal procedures to go through. As if to add insult to injury, I was informed that I had to face an interview with the police just three days after Maggie's death. She had gone over Beachy Head but had left no note, and there had been no witnesses.

'Nobody saw her die,' a policeman explained to me. 'As part of our procedure we need to ask you some questions. I'm sorry, Mr Lane, but we don't know whether you were the cause of your wife's death.' The police began to grill me as though I were a criminal. I was faced with a barrage of questions, some of them incredibly personal. I was gobsmacked and repulsed.

They asked me what our sex life was like. Had the sex gone off? Had we been fighting? Was I physical with her? Did I beat her? Was the relationship awful? Had I been driven to the point where I could have killed her?

Having to rake over everything in such a way, and so soon after Maggie had died, was almost too much to bear. Nevertheless, I answered all their questions. My distress must have been pretty obvious, because after some time the police cut it off suddenly.

'Don't worry, Mr Lane,' they said. 'We know you're innocent, but we always have to push people until we're sure one way or the other. We have to report back and be able to say, "That man did not kill his wife" to our superiors.'

It was obvious the police felt bad about what they had to put me through, and looking back I can completely understand it all. They were only doing their job.

Once the possibility of murder had been eliminated, they were left with the option of suicide or 'open verdict'. It would be another six months, after Maggie's case finally went to court, before an open verdict about her death was reached. Why? Because no one saw her go and there was no note.

CHAPTER 5

A VISIT TO
THE EDGE

People tell you the best way to deal with grief is to get on with things and in the days between Maggie's death and her funeral that's exactly what I tried to do. For the odd hour or two every day I tried to go back to doing the job I make my living from – cleaning windows.

One morning, around 5 am, I was on a job in Mead Street when I had a sudden urge to go up to Beachy Head. I hadn't even thought about going up since Maggie had been found, but now the compulsion was so strong that I simply had to. Perhaps I was experiencing a sort of car crash mentality – you feel you just have to look. Even though I knew it would be painful, I left my work and set off right away.

I had no idea where Maggie had been found. Beachy Head is a large area of headland and as I drove I realised I didn't even know where Maggie had fallen. Nevertheless, I drove on and pulled into the first car park I found. I turned off the engine and stared out at the vast expanse of grass that leads up to the cliffs.

A woman came into view. She was walking along a pathway and was close enough for me to see that she was crying. Immediately I felt that something must be wrong. It was barely 5.30 am. What was this woman doing up here? Right away, I thought the worst – that she was going to kill herself – and after a few moments, I decided to follow her. Until I'd spotted the woman, I'd been in my own world of grief and emotion. Now I was focused suddenly, my feelings about Maggie temporarily switched off.

The woman had disappeared around a corner. Once I turned the same corner, I realised she was a surprisingly long way ahead of me and walking quite fast, though nowhere near the cliff yet. Still, I was concerned – she'd been crying.

Before I caught up with her, she sat down on a bench quite near the cliff. As I walked towards the bench, I could see that she was in her mid-30s and that she was writing a note – it turned out to be a suicide note.

I decided to sit down beside her. She said nothing. I had to say something.

'I hope you aren't going to do what I think you're going to do, sweetheart,' I began slowly, calmly.

'What's it got to do with you?' she snapped back. Plainly,

she wasn't glad of my company. Perhaps she had a point. Perhaps it didn't have anything to do with me.

'Do you realise why I'm up here?' I asked her. She shook her head slightly.

'I'm trying to come to terms with my wife dying up here a week ago,' I continued.

'Well, you know what I'm going to do, then,' she replied. 'And I've got a right to do it!'

'No you don't, sweetheart, you...'

I couldn't carry on speaking. I just burst into tears. I couldn't believe this was happening. Barely a week after Maggie's death, I was sitting with another woman who was about to commit suicide. The thought of Maggie, the thought of this lady, the thought of her family... the sadness of it all was overwhelming.

I began to try and convince her that whatever her problems, suicide was not the answer. But she didn't listen to me for long. Before I knew it she had got up and begun to run. There was about 100 yards between the bench and the cliff edge and she already had a head start. I sprang from my seat and ran like I'd never run before. The adrenaline made me fly along and soon I was gaining on her, just as she was gaining on the cliff edge. The edge loomed closer and closer and I'd nearly caught up with her by the time she was about 3 feet from it. It's now or never, I thought, as I threw myself through the air with all my might.

I brought her down with a rugby tackle. A second later and she would have been gone.

I yanked her away from the edge, jumped on top of her and tried to hold her still. It wasn't easy – the strength of a desperate person is phenomenal – but so is the strength of a person who is desperate to save someone, and I managed to keep her down.

In the distance I could see the police – I later learned they were looking for the very person I had wrestled to the ground – and began trying to wave while keeping a firm grip on the woman. Unlikely as it may seem – and unfortunately for me – the police thought we were a courting couple because I was on top of her and they passed us by at first!

The woman began to scream at me, repeating, 'I want to die, I want to die!' over and over. I had no idea how to calm her down. All I could do was keep on struggling with her as she writhed beneath me.

Then, suddenly, she stopped fighting.

Her body went limp, she stopped screaming and looked at me straight in the eye. 'Why don't you and I go over hand in hand?' she said, her tone flat and cold, her eyes icy.

Her words sent a shiver down my spine, and for a few moments I was so spooked that I nearly lost my grip. A few weeks before she died, Maggie had woken me up to tell me about a bad dream. She had dreamt that we'd fallen over Beachy Head together – *hand in hand*. Those were the words Maggie had used and those were the words I was hearing now. When Maggie had spoken them, I was shaken rigid.

50

Now, hearing them again, I was petrified. I thought it was a calling from Maggie for me to join her.

'No way,' I shouted, regaining my grip. 'I'm not ready to die yet. I'm not going with you and you're staying where you are. *I'm not letting you go.*'

By now the police had begun to suspect that we weren't a loving couple, and were running towards us. They took hold of the woman, but I could see her continuing to fight like a tiger as they tried to walk her down the hill.

There was no way they could get her in the car. The more they tried, the more she struggled. I could see it was a futile exercise – the woman was only getting more and more upset, so after a few minutes I shouted, 'Hold it, just hold it a second!'

The police paused and so did the woman. I looked right into her teary eyes –mine were teary too, because the situation was so emotional. 'Look,' I said gently, 'if I come with you to the police station, will you come quietly? I'll come with you as far as I'm allowed, I promise. Do you understand?'

It was as if I was saying what I would have said to Maggie had I found her up there a week before.

She looked a little bemused, but nodded. 'Yes, if you come with me, I'll go quietly,' she said after a while.

The police breathed a sigh of relief as we got into the back of the car. It was so strange to be hugging and crying with a complete stranger as the police drove us to the station. When we arrived, they let me come in with her. I held her hand while the police went through their procedures. I constantly reassured her that she was not under arrest, but was only going to be questioned and kept in a cell for her own safety. I told her that she would be treated kindly so long as she cooperated, which she did.

Finally, it was time for me to go. I'd done all I could. The woman was in the hands of the police now. As I went to leave, she blew me a kiss.

I stepped out of the police station into the morning air and suddenly the strangeness of the whole episode hit me. Why did I get that urge to go up to Beachy Head? I wondered. It felt like an uncanny coincidence that I had stumbled across this desperate, lonely soul and saved her. It was quite a traumatic thing to have experienced so soon after Maggie's death, but I knew I'd done the right thing by following her up the hill. If someone had been there last week, I thought, then Maggie would still be alive today.

And that's when the idea came to me – patrols along Beachy Head were needed at all times to stop this sort of thing happening. People should be up there 24 hours a day. I had been told that there was some sort of patrolling in place, but I had never seen anyone up there and I knew there was certainly not 24-hour cover. From that moment on, my campaign to achieve that goal began.

The next day I paid a visit to the woman I'd dragged back from the Head. She had been sectioned under the Mental Health Act, which allows people to be detained if they are perceived as a danger to themselves, and I was taken to her room in the hospital's psychiatric wing. When I walked in, I didn't receive the friendliest of welcomes.

'You bastard,' she shouted, 'all I wanted to do was die and you stopped me!'

She continued before I could respond, this time lowering her voice. 'I'm going to be a good girl in here and when I get out I'm going to kill myself!' she said, quietly but angrily.

I didn't know quite how to respond. I'm no psychologist or counsellor, and I wasn't trained to know the 'right thing' to say to someone in such distress. But instead of worrying, I simply said what came naturally to me.

'Come on,' I began, 'why don't you just talk to me instead of shouting? Have you really thought about what you're doing – do you realise what you're going to do to your family if you kill yourself?'

'My family hate me,' she retorted. 'My son and daughter can't stand me and think I'm a nutcase. They never see me.'

It was hard to get through to her. I visited her four times. Each time we talked about how determined she was to kill herself and each time I became more determined to change her way of thinking. I described my pain over Maggie, I showed her Maggie's photos, all in the hope that I could get through to her, make her feel her life was worth something both to her and others. The conversation often turned back to her family.

'They don't love me,' she'd say, flatly.

'Have you tried calling them?' I asked, in response. 'Why don't you try and open up the lines of communication again and just see if they really do hate you? I think you might be wrong about that.'

It was no use. Her stock response was: 'I ain't ringing them.'

The fifth time I visited I learned that she'd been discharged. Considering what she'd been saying to me, I wasn't sure this was a good thing, but I'd already begun patrolling up and down Beachy Head when I wasn't organising Maggie's funeral or dealing with other matters. I was worried. I'd keep my eye out for her.

Three months later, I was strolling through the Arndale Shopping Centre in Eastbourne when a woman approached me. Her face was familiar but I couldn't pin it down right away. It wasn't until she began speaking that I twigged who it was.

'I just want to thank you very much for saving my life,' she said, smiling. 'I took your advice and phoned my kids, and now I see them every week. I've got my own flat too – my life's back on track!'

Wow, I thought. I did the right thing. It warmed my heart to know that I had helped – and I knew there was more to be done.

*   *   *

I may have been innocent of killing Maggie in the eyes of the law, but in the days following her death I didn't feel that way myself.

54

Even though the last words we ever spoke were 'I love you', and although no matter how bad things got we never went to sleep without saying those words, I felt as if I had condemned Maggie to die. I turned it over and over in my head – If I'd gone home that lunchtime, she'd be alive today, I reasoned. I could have saved her. It was my fault that she was dead.

Sometimes I still have those thoughts, though now I know they are wrong. I didn't condemn Maggie to death by not going home. Sure, if I'd gone to meet her I may have prevented her from doing what she did that day, but there's a good chance that I would merely have been delaying the inevitable – and it makes me very sad to say that.

At the time, however, my mind was all over the place and I was convinced it was all down to failure on my part. I felt guilty and numb with disbelief. I could not believe what had happened. As I walked around the house, staring at the photos of Maggie that lay on every surface, I found it impossible to accept that she was never going to walk through our front door once more. I would sit for hours and stare at the smile that drew me to her in the first place, trying to absorb the fact that I would never see it spread across her face again.

I would constantly open her wardrobe and look at the clothes she used to wear on our evenings out; I'd open her perfume just to smell her again. I'd go to her pillow and hold it to my face, desperate to get close to whatever remained of her. I'd play our favourite songs, look at her wedding photos and then eventually I'd fall asleep on the sofa. For a long time, it would take me a few moments after waking before I realised that Maggie wasn't lying beside me and that I was waking up to a life that should have been a bad dream.

Before the funeral, a very strange thing happened to me. I was sitting indoors, wide awake, yet quite suddenly my vision misted over and I couldn't see. After a few moments, the mist began to clear slightly and all I could see was Beachy Head. I was standing by the cliff edge. (It wasn't until weeks later, when the coroner took me up to Beachy Head that I realised the spot I was visualising now was the very spot Maggie had fallen from.) I was looking back towards the car park and to Maggie's car. Maggie was in her black-and-white outfit, walking up the hill towards me. She came closer and closer, until she was within an inch of me – and then she walked right into me. *She was right inside me…* Suddenly I'm her and I'm falling over the cliff, but instead of going down I fly up and become me again. Looking over my shoulder from my position up in the air, I see Maggie's body going over the cliff and down and I hear her calling: 'Don't worry, the angels are coming to get me,' she cries out. 'I didn't suffer. My body went down there, but I went up there where you are!'

I was floating, looking down at her body for a few moments, and then my eyes cleared. I blinked and looked around the living room, shaking like a leaf. I was drenched in sweat from head to toe.

I hardly knew what to make of it, but I believed that this vision was a sign of Maggie somehow making contact with me. I'd never had a spiritual experience before, but I've no doubt that this was one. I was sure that Maggie was trying to help me; that she knew she'd hurt me badly and that I was blaming myself for her death. My vision came before the funeral and it gave me enough strength – just about – to hold myself together and get through the day.

Maggie and I had always been open with each other. We'd talked about what we wanted for our funerals should one of us die. Now she was gone, there was no way I was going to do it any way other than how she'd wanted it. Making the arrangements was the only thing I was able to apply myself to in those blurry few days. I was living from moment to moment through the chaos of emotional ups and downs. I felt capable of nothing and cared about very little, but one thing I knew I had to get right was the funeral.

'I don't want lots of flowers,' Maggie had told me. There would be no flowers.

'I only want one orchid.' Then there would only be one.

'And I want it to be placed on the coffin.' So that's where it was placed.

'There are to be no prayers and the only reading is to be written and read by you, Keith.'

Before we arrived at the church, 'Tears from Heaven' by Eric Clapton was playing and the only other music was to be Ronan Keating's version of the Garth Brooks song 'If

Tomorrow Never Comes', and the Toni Braxton song, 'Breathe Again' that we both loved dearly – I'd often kneel on the floor at home and sing it to Maggie while she laughed her head off!

On the day of the funeral, the coffin was brought in while 'Breathe Again' played, and once it had been put down I stood up to do my reading. If identifying Maggie's body was the hardest thing I have ever done, then that reading was the second hardest. I conveyed my love for Maggie to a room of mourners and only just managed to hold it together. I began to choke up with tears towards the end, but 'If Tomorrow Never Comes' began to play as I finished speaking and it gave me the crutch that I needed. I turned around to face Maggie's coffin, and I sang every word at the top of my voice, as if I was performing for her on our settee again.

Tears ran down my cheeks as I sang my heart out to Maggie, and as the song ended I blew her a kiss and said, 'Goodbye, my darling.'

It was the only thing left to say.

CHAPTER 6

BACK AT
THE EDGE

In the days leading up to Maggie's funeral, I had been surrounded by a swarm of friends and family. Now the funeral was over and things were different. People had to go back to their lives and I had to go back to mine. The only problem was that the life I had to go back to was a life I hardly wanted any more. There was a massive Maggie-shaped void bang in the middle of it.

I could hardly eat, I could hardly sleep and I felt more alone than ever. What do I do now? I thought. How could I possibly get over this? There seemed to be no answer. I was horribly alone.

Nevertheless, there was something I had to do and I began to do it obsessively. With Maggie and the woman I'd saved in mind, I began to patrol the cliffs at Beachy Head two or three times a day. I was on a mission to stop what had happened to Maggie (and me) happening to others.

At first I was frightened – paranoid, even – that every person I saw up there was out to kill themselves. I'd approach anyone I saw near the edge and ask them if they were OK. A lot of people looked at me as if I was crazy. After all, Beachy Head is known be favoured by suicides but it's also an outstanding beauty spot, popular with all manner of people who go up there to enjoy it. It's a wonder there weren't any serious complaints about the nutter who kept asking anyone and everyone if they were thinking of jumping!

Luckily, the locals understood the problems up there and were very kind. Most of the time people simply said 'Keep up the good work' after I'd explained what I was doing and any confusion had been cleared up. Some people did retreat quite hastily, though. At that point I hadn't the experience to recognise the body language of those who were contemplating death. Neither had I learned quite how to approach people. It would be a steep learning curve.

I was patrolling one day a few weeks after the funeral. It was a beautiful sunny day in late April and the headland was dotted with people enjoying the fine weather and the gentle breeze that carried the calls of seagulls soaring above.

In the middle of all this, I spotted something strange. There was a man sitting at the cliff edge. Nothing unusual about that, you may think, and you'd be right. But as I got closer I noticed that his legs were dangling over the edge of the cliff. Now, this was unusual – most people would not casually let their legs hang over a drop like that.

He was clutching something to his chest and staring out to sea. I walked over to him, close enough to see the tears that were rolling down his cheeks. I knew the moment had come – I had a major problem on my hands. I didn't think much about exactly how to deal with it. Instead of getting bogged down with worry I simply walked up to him, sat myself down, put my legs over the edge and joined him in staring out to sea.

It was then that I realised I had this man's life in my hands. We sat in silence, and neither of us moved a muscle for a few moments. The man seemed oblivious to me – it was as if I wasn't even there.

I didn't want to use a 'You're not going to jump, are you?' approach – he was far too close to the edge for that – there was nothing I could do to stop him if he decided to go. Instead, I spoke to him as if I hadn't even realised he was in trouble.

'Wow, some view we've got here, isn't it?' I began, my voice friendly and a little jolly. I didn't look at him, but just waited.

'Hmmm,' he replied, sniffling a little as he tried to stop crying.

'What a beautiful place,' I continued. 'You from around here?'

'No,' he said simply.

I looked sideways at him. His eyes were fixed on the horizon. He looked focused, in a world of his own, staring out and clutching what I could now see was a picture frame.

'What picture have you got there then?' I asked.

'It's my daughters,' he replied. He looked so very melancholic.

'Really?' I answered, enthusiastically. 'Can I have a look?'

I was desperate not to make him think I suspected him of anything. I wanted him to think I was simply curious about his picture. It was almost farcical, but for the moment it seemed to be working. He hadn't jumped yet, after all.

He handed me the picture frame, which contained a photo of two lovely-looking young kids of around three and six years old.

'Wow!' I exclaimed. 'What beautiful children you've got!'

That's when he turned to look at me. I'd made contact, I'd broken through, and it was a relief. Tears were still streaming down his face. He said nothing, but just looked at me, helpless and lost.

'You're not OK, are you?' I said softly.

'No…'

'With such beautiful children at home, I do hope you're not thinking of going over the edge,' I continued carefully. I paused for a few moments and then added, 'Are you?'

'Well, yes,' he said hesitantly, as if he were in a great amount of pain, 'I am.'

I knew that now I'd made eye contact, now I'd shown him I cared, it was my chance to try and talk him down.

'I don't know your circumstances,' I said to him, careful to maintain eye contact, 'but all I can tell you is that I lost my wife here and it's been the most devastating thing in the world. Nobody could have prepared me for this amount of pain. Could you put your wonderful kids through that?'

He was listening, he wasn't making any moves, so I carried on.

'Should you die, your eldest will know what's going on even if your youngest doesn't. And when they're older, both of them are going to want the answers to a lot of questions about why they've grown up without a dad. Can you really imagine those kids growing up without their father? Can you imagine someone else meeting your wife and bringing your children up? Can you really do this?'

Suddenly he burst into heavy tears. 'No,' he cried, 'You're right, I can't. You're absolutely right.'

It's hard to describe the sense of relief I felt on hearing those words. I knew he was safe. 'I don't think you want to do it at all, do you?' I said consolingly.

He shook his head, and cried a little more.

'Come on,' I said, 'let's get you away from the edge. In fact, let's go and have a coffee, or even a beer.'

I put my arm around him, got him up and walked him down the hill, and all the while he was clutching the frame that contained his precious daughters. We got to the Beachy

Head Pub, sat down for a pint and it was only then that he let it all out.

He'd split with his wife and was having problems gaining access to his kids. He felt like he was losing them. His wife had the house so that she could look after them and he had moved out and was living in digs. He felt his life had gone from pretty normal to a complete mess, and didn't think he had anything left to live for.

It wasn't his problems that struck me as *the problem*, though – it was the fact that he evidently hadn't had the chance to really talk to anyone about them. Even telling a complete stranger what he was going through seemed to help him begin to put things into perspective. I gave him some advice, urging him to make sure he stayed in touch with his children and to find a good solicitor. I did my best to reassure him that however things turned out between him and his wife, he could still be a great dad and play a vital role in his kids' upbringing.

By the time we'd finished our pint, I felt as if I was chatting to a different person. The tears had stopped, and we were both talking practically about how he could sort out his situation.

Afterwards, I waited with him until his bus came – I wanted to make sure he got away from the area. As he got on, I told him to keep looking at the picture and that I didn't want to see him at Beachy Head again.

'You won't,' he said, and smiled.

64

I could hardly believe that it had happened again. This man was the second person I'd helped in a very short space of time, which meant that two families would not have to live through the hell that Maggie's death plunged me into. I felt a slight sense of elation as I walked away after I'd said goodbye. Deep down I felt that I'd done something right again, and that my decision to patrol the cliffs was a good one. When I'd spotted the man, I hadn't applied a method to saving him. Rather, I'd gone with the flow and let my instinct dictate how I tackled the situation. I decided there and then that this would be my *modus operandi* in future.

*   *   *

Even though I was patrolling every day, I still didn't know which spot Maggie had fallen from. To find out, I had to wait for the coroner's report to be released. It was a long wait, around seven weeks. But sure enough, soon after the report came out, the coroner agreed to show me where my wife had died.

I had made a little wooden cross to mark the spot and I took it with me to meet the coroner.

It was a misty day, so much so that we could hardly see our hands in front of our faces as we climbed Beachy Head. The quietness that comes with fog gave the place an eerie feel and as we climbed I felt slightly frightened.

When the coroner had pulled up at the car park she had been a bit reluctant to go up, but I'd persuaded her and agreed that if the fog got too bad we would come down. After a few minutes of climbing, the mist cleared enough for the coroner to search the area. I followed her nervously, cross in hand.

'Ah,' she exclaimed suddenly, 'it's just here.'

I went cold. At last I was standing by the spot where Maggie had spent her final moments. I can hardly put into words how much my mind raced. A hundred images flashed through my head at once – each one a different take on how she might have met her end. I pictured her jumping, slipping, grabbing, falling one way and then another, hitting the cliff, bouncing, screaming – the agony of it was that I had no clue which version of events was the right one *and I knew I would never find out*. I swooned with all those thoughts for some minutes until I felt the cross in my hand and snapped out of it – I wasn't here to drive myself crazy, I was here to mark Maggie's spot with the cross I'd made.

The point Maggie fell from isn't a sheer drop to start with. The cliff edge curves away, gently at first, until it begins to steepen towards the vertical chalk. I had a firm idea where Maggie must have gone over, and resolved to place the cross just there.

Slowly, I inched down towards where the cliff began to fall away. Obviously I wasn't doing what the coroner had expected I'd be doing, for she started going berserk.

'For God's sake, Keith, come back,' she shouted. 'If you bloody well go over, my job's on the line!'

There was no way I was going back, though, and I told her so. I carried on inching down and once I'd gone about 10 feet, I hammered the cross in. It was the right place for it – there was no chance of anyone stumbling on or stealing it unless they were crackers enough to climb down for it. As soon as I'd finished I scrambled back up – much to the relief of the coroner, poor woman!

I turned to look down at the cross and spoke to Maggie. 'Well, sweetheart,' I began, 'I'm not going to say goodbye because I'm going to be here every day now. I'm going to make this place safe, so don't you worry about that.'

CHAPTER 7

A DOWNWARD SPIRAL AND A GLIMMER OF HOPE

Grief is a strange thing. The journey after bereavement is full of twists and turns, and everyone experiences it in different ways. Counsellors will tell you that there different stages of grief and anger, and they're right, but each individual has to find their own way through the mess of losing someone. Looking back, I can see that beginning my patrols was as much a part of my grief over losing Maggie as it was about helping others. Put simply, at first I was driven to be up there and it helped me in some way, just as it helped the people I talked to.

In those early days and months back in 2004, the time I spent up at the Head managed to focus my mind a little. Just a little. But each day, when I returned home, I was also returning to a dark, deeply depressing place in my mind.

I didn't want to be at home and be reminded of Maggie, yet I didn't want to be out facing other people. I didn't want to be awake, yet I couldn't sleep. And when I woke up in the morning, I didn't want to get out of bed and face another day. To me, the world had become a strange, grey place and I felt like an alien living in it. Being conscious merely reminded me of how difficult life had become, and only made me feel more isolated. As I walked around, I felt like an empty shell – and an angry, empty shell to boot.

When you're so down, you become very focused on yourself and lose the ability to see things as they are. To me, everyone in the world seemed happy apart for me, and I didn't know what on earth I could do to help myself. Why is everyone else smiling? I'd think. No one gives a shit that Maggie's dead, no one cares about me and the world's just going on as if nothing's happened.

As time went on, my thoughts became even darker: I began to feel that everyone was looking at me because I was the man in the newspaper whose wife had died. Looking back, I'm sure they weren't, but at the time I was convinced of it and I began to shut down. I didn't want to eat, I only wanted to sleep and be away from it all. I wanted some peace from my thoughts of Maggie, and being unconscious was the only real answer. But I couldn't sleep forever, so every day I faced the same question: 'How am I going to get through the next 24 hours?'

I was prescribed Prozac. My GP had been close to Maggie

and was devastated when he heard she had died. There was no way he was going to let me go the same way, so he kept a close eye on me. Dr Ribbons was absolutely brilliant. I was reluctant to take the pills, but they proved invaluable as a crutch to get through the day. They didn't make the pain go away, but they allowed me to function on a very basic level. Without those pills, I think there's a good chance I would have taken my own life.

Maggie and I had been with each other 24/7 and now it was just me. I could hardly work any more, the debts were piling up and I was beginning to really struggle.

I didn't know who to turn to. At first, everyone had been so very kind, asking after me and offering to help all the time. But people are only human, and after a while they get bored of helping others if they don't feel their help is – well – *helping*. After all, I didn't show many signs of improvement. I soon began to notice that the people who had been so keen to look out for me before were now crossing the street to avoid me. In the pub, friends would try to turn their backs subtly when I walked in – just from the looks on their faces, I could see they were thinking, Crikey here comes Misery Guts again, with nothing to say apart from how much he misses his wife. The thing is, this was all perfectly understandable. People want to get on with their lives – they go out to be happy, not sad. I understand that now, and I understood it then, but it doesn't change the fact that it only made me feel more alone at the time.

I knew I could call my family if I needed them, but I also knew – or at least, I felt – that I was a burden. The fact was that I didn't like myself very much, and didn't expect myself to be liked. I felt I was one big pain in the arse, both to myself and others. Everyone knows the saying, 'Laugh and the world laughs with you.' Well, the flipside of that is, 'Cry and no one gives a monkey's!'

I felt dead inside. I was quite literally dying of a broken heart. And then I began to drink again.

I'd cut out booze after Maggie died. I knew it was what had killed her and I just didn't want it in my life. But time wore on, and two or three months later I began having a few whiskies at home, which turned into a few more whiskies and before I knew it I was knocking myself out with the stuff virtually every night of the week. Being depressed draws you to drink – alcohol gives you a temporary lift, but ironically ends up making you even more depressed. It's what happened to Maggie, and I suppose it's what was happening to me.

Even though I was sinking into a downward spiral, nothing could stop me from going up to Beachy Head each morning. It was the only routine I had left. I was up there seven days a week without fail, starting at 5.30 in the morning. Each day, I parked my car at the car park, walked up to the highest point and, using my binoculars, looked along the cliffs to see if there was anyone standing at the edge. If there was no one around, I'd look over the edge to see if anyone had gone over – by this stage a Christian organisation called the Beachy Head Chaplaincy Team had begun patrolling the cliffs from 6 pm 'til midnight, but I was always concerned that somebody may have killed themselves during the hours between the chaplains finishing their patrol and me starting mine. I was obsessive about checking because in the early days I took it very personally if a person went over. It made me feel like I had failed.

One warm June morning, I was patrolling as usual at around 7 am and noticed a man sitting on the grass near the edge. Because erosion is causing the cliff edge to fall into the sea bit by bit, there are parts of the cliff that look like little steps and can act as benches to people who don't suffer from vertigo. The man was reading a paper on one of them. It was a warm morning, for sure, but it struck me as a little odd that someone would be up on a cliff so early just to catch up with the news. Certainly, it was the first time I'd seen anyone do it. I wanted to give him the benefit of the doubt, though, so I decided to observe him discreetly rather than rush up and interrupt him.

I walked past him from behind. Sure enough, nothing seemed amiss. I carried on walking for a few minutes, turned, and began to make my way back to the bench. As I walked past him again, I noticed that he wasn't reading the paper at all. He was staring over the top of it. What's more, I noticed that he hadn't turned the page in five minutes. So either he was a very slow reader or something wasn't quite right.

I sat down on the same ledge and remarked on what a nice day it was. Then I asked him casually if he was feeling OK.

'Yes, why shouldn't I be?' he replied, very matter-of-factly. Perhaps I'd made a mistake. Perhaps I was merely disturbing this man's peace and quiet. Still, I'd disturbed it now, so why not carry on for a bit? I would rather have discovered I was being a nuisance than have passed by a potential jumper.

I told him about my patrols, and about Maggie. I always mentioned Maggie because, nine times out of ten, her story caught people's attention and made them concentrate, irrespective of whether they had a problem or not. You can teach people all sorts of things, but you can't teach them experience and my experience always seemed to give me some kind of authority. Whether or not my story inspired respect, empathy or merely made people inquisitive, they seemed to want to listen to it and that was good enough for me.

The man seemed moved by my words, and said he was sorry about what I'd been through. His concern for me made me begin to think that I was really barking up the wrong tree with this one. Still, I had one more question for him.

'When I walked past you just now I noticed you weren't turning the pages of your newspaper. Please forgive me if I'm intruding on you at all but...'

Tears began to form in his eyes.

'You have got a problem, haven't you?' I continued.

He nodded.

'Thought so,' I said. 'Do you want to talk about it? After all, a problem shared is a problem halved. Believe me, I understand how you feel. You feel like you're in a tunnel with no light at the end of it, don't you? That's how I feel now I've lost my wife.'

'You're right,' he said, looking at me a little more directly.

'I'm not asking you to walk away from here,' I assured him. 'All I'm offering you is a shoulder to cry on. Why don't we talk about it? You never know, you might have second thoughts about doing what you're thinking of doing.'

At this, the man began to speak. He explained that his wife of forty years had died six months ago and that he was in Eastbourne on holiday with his second wife. He had remarried quite quickly, but there was a major problem in his new relationship: his new wife wouldn't allow any of his first wife's photos in the house. She wouldn't let him talk about her, and wouldn't let him share anything about her. By the time he finished telling his story, he was in floods of tears. I put my arm around him, and told him it was OK to cry.

'You haven't had time to reflect and grieve, have you?' I asked.

'No, not at all.' He loved his new wife very much, but it didn't mean he was 'over' losing the woman he'd spent 40 years with. 'Bloody hell,' he said, 'I'm glad my new wife's not up here to see this!'

It was obvious how much emotion this guy had been holding back.

'You've had a great loss, and you're not being allowed to get it all out. Have you tried talking to your new wife about your feelings?'

'I'm frightened that – if I tried to – we might have a row,' he said. 'I don't want to push her away.'

'That's understandable,' I said, 'but surely *this* isn't a perfect situation. Who knows, if you are open with your wife, if you explain everything and reassure her that you love her but that you also need to grieve, she may understand. It could even bring you closer…'

He nodded slowly. Yes, I thought, he's starting to see things differently. It was time to get him away from the edge.

'Come on,' I smiled. 'Put that paper down and let's go over to the pub and have a coffee.'

He didn't take any persuading. We walked away, took a seat in the Beachy Head Pub for a while and then said goodbye once we got back to his car.

We shook hands and for a moment I thought he was going to shake mine off! He was smiling and had a look of resolve in his eyes. I could tell he intended to finally address the situation that had brought him so much anguish.

'Good luck,' I said.

'Thank you for what you've done,' he beamed. 'And keep up the good work!'

He let go of my hand, and off he went.

Blimey, I thought once he'd gone, where did all those words of advice come from? I was elated again, for sure, but

I couldn't fathom quite how I'd managed to talk in that way. I'd always been a helper and a carer and family members had often come to me with their troubles because I'm a good listener. But I'd never been known for handing out advice so... fluently. The words I spoke to that man had rolled off my tongue and as I was talking I had a sense that I didn't know quite where they were coming from. I hadn't had time to reflect and consider – to think before I spoke – yet words that were able to stop a man from killing himself had fallen spontaneously from my mouth. It seemed to good to be true. Perhaps it had been the pressure of the moment, I thought. Maybe when humans are faced with extreme situations where lives are at stake, something in the brain kicks in and the right words just flow.

But something else occurred to me. Maybe they weren't all my words. Maybe I was being helped. That day was the first time I thought that someone was guiding me in those moments. And that someone was Maggie.

*   *   *

I'd saved three people in a short space of time, and I was very happy about it. But it was all I was happy about. When I wasn't patrolling, I was still a total mess. I may have spent my time up there talking to people about their problems, but when I came down I wasn't talking to anyone about mine. I tried going to a counsellor, but raking over my feelings about losing Maggie made things worse. The fact was that she was gone, and there wasn't anything I – or anyone else – could say to bring her back or help me feel better.

When I felt up to it, I was doing window-cleaning jobs here and there. One day, I was working in a customer's garden – and feeling really terrible. My mind wasn't really on the job and my emotions were all over the place as I cleaned. I could feel myself welling up, so I climbed down from my ladder. Not wanting to be defeated by my feelings and simply go home, I went to the bottom of the garden and into the customer's shed to avoid being seen, and once I was there I began to cry uncontrollably. I couldn't stop. It seemed that, no matter what I did – work, patrolling, trying to get on with things – the pain just wouldn't go away. Crying in that shed, I felt as if my heart was going to burst out of my body. God I missed Maggie. My life meant nothing without her by my side.

My customer must have noticed I was gone and heard me crying. She opened the shed door and put her arms around me.

'If you want to cry, just cry,' she said. She didn't question what was wrong – she must have read about me in the local papers.

'I think you need to see somebody,' she said after a couple of minutes. 'I've got a friend and I'm going to give you her number. She's a spiritualist.'

Spiritualist? I thought. My God, what good will a spiritualist be to me? I looked up at my customer, unsure of what she meant.

'Don't knock it,' she said. 'Just trust me and phone her.'

Why not? I thought. I was willing to try anything if it might help me out of the hell I was in. I took the number for the spiritualist, someone called Jules, and went home for the day.

I made the call. A woman answered and I gave her my name and the name of my customer. I told her my story and asked if she thought she might be able to help. She listened but told me she was taking a break at the moment in order to attend to some personal matters in her own life. She was sorry, but explained that giving up time for others was just too draining for her.

Great. So that was that. We said goodbye and my heart sank.

Thirty seconds later, my phone rang. It was Jules.

'I'm calling you back because as soon as I put down the phone, the spirits were telling me that I had to help this man, that it is my duty. I must see you as soon as possible.'

Blimey, I thought, Now *that* is a result! We agreed to meet that very evening. I can't say I wasn't sceptical. After all, I'd never really believed in spirits, and apart from the brief moments I've already described, I'd never experienced anything that you could really call a 'spiritual experience'. But I decided to go along with an open mind.

The moment I met Jules I felt a wonderful sense of comfort. She had an aura of wisdom and calm that put me at ease immediately. As we talked in her lounge, I found myself opening up in a way that I hadn't done with anybody since Maggie's death. I was like putty in her hands – she seemed to know how to relax me and draw me out of myself in a very natural way.

Jules said that she had heard from the spirits and that Maggie would be making contact, but not yet. My departed wife had only just crossed over to the other side and wasn't quite ready.

It's easy to dismiss the idea of spirits and spirituality as mumbo jumbo. I'd done it myself in the past. But listening to Jules now, I had a sense that she was speaking from the heart. This wasn't some palm reader trying to make a buck at a fun fair – Jules wasn't making any promises or giving me false hope. She was merely asking me to have faith that Maggie would eventually make contact.

I was very aware that my desperate position meant I might have been more willing than usual to clutch at straws. But at the same time I could not completely dismiss the possibility that spirits exists and that Maggie may want to get in touch. I can't say I had faith straight away. Rather, because of my situation, I *wanted* to have faith, I *wanted* to hang on to something – anything. If there was even the remotest chance that I would be able to have some contact with my Maggie again, I was willing to give it a go. So I decided to suspend any lingering disbelief and go with the flow. My world had become a very dark place, but now I had a glimmer of hope.

I started to see Jules once a week. Every time we met, I felt the same sense of calm and comfort, which was good in itself, and she and I quickly became good friends. During every session, Jules told me where Maggie was, but that she was still not ready to make contact. I had to have faith. It wasn't easy to keep believing, but I did. And as later, amazing events proved, I was right to persevere...

Despite that glimmer of hope, I was still very delicate emotionally. As the days and weeks passed I felt like I was falling into a black hole that I couldn't pull back from. I kept telling myself that life would get better, that I just needed to hold on, keep going and muddle through until the misery started to wane. But I was so depressed that I could hardly believe what I was telling myself. The strain of living was dragging me down.

Then, one night, I decided I'd had enough of everything. I decided to go up to Beachy Head.

I was completely smashed. I'd downed a bottle of vodka at home and ordered a taxi. I took a little stool with me in the cab, which seemed to go unnoticed, and once the cabbie dropped me off I began stumbling up the hill. It was pitch black and I had no torch. With the logic of a drunk I decided it would be a good idea to sit on my stool and talk to the full moon before throwing myself over the edge from Maggie's spot. There was one problem, however. I was so drunk that I couldn't find it in the darkness! I look back and laugh at the whole plan now, but at the time it was far from funny.

I flailed around, desperately searching for Maggie's cross. I was perilously close to the edge and so drunk that I ended up on my stomach in the pitch black, feeling around for the right place, hoping I'd end up with the cross in my hand. I must have been inches from slipping away forever.

Then, something triggered in my brain. In a moment of clarity I became painfully aware of the finality of what I was about to do – and that I shouldn't be doing it. I was at the place where I would normally be persuading people not to die and asking them if it was what they really wanted; now I had to answer that question myself. Seconds earlier I'd been hell-bent on ending it all, but now I was overwhelmed by one thought: I didn't want to die.

I needed to be away from there. I needed to be safe and I needed help. Drunkenly, I pulled out my mobile phone and spoke to Jules. I told her where I was, but that there was no need to worry: I was coming down but I needed to talk to someone.

I began to stumble back down the hill towards the road. I'd decided to head home, but I was so drunk I could hardly focus on what was in front of me. As I stumbled down the road, stool in hand, I must have been quite a sorry sight!

The next thing I knew, two police cars had screeched to a halt in front of me. It turned out that Jules had been so worried about me falling from the cliff that she'd called the police. Now I was facing two police officers wanting to know what on earth I was doing – and wondering what the stool was for!

'Don't worry about that,' I slurred, 'I'm not going to jump. I'm 500 feet from the edge now and I can't jump 501 feet!'

With that they threw me in the back of the car. I think they knew I was in a state and they couldn't take any chances that I might do something stupid. Back at the station I was questioned until they were satisfied I wasn't going to kill myself, and then released.

I wasn't proud of myself, and I had to think long and hard about what I'd done. Looking back, I can see that my actions were little more than a cry for help. I went up to the Head with the intention of killing myself, but I don't think it was *real* intention. In the years that followed I would meet many people who really had the intention and who could not be stopped, but I didn't fall into that category. I think it just took me getting to the cliff edge to realise that I didn't want to die. Rather, I wanted help; I wanted some kind of way out.

I was in such a desperate place in my mind. Because of my Beachy Head work, and the drugs, I was keeping just above the water line – bobbing along in a leaky boat but not quite sinking, and this episode marked my lowest point. It was the first time I had contemplated suicide. I couldn't have got any lower. When you're that bad, it's natural to end up seeking attention. Humans need other humans, and unconsciously I was trying to reach out and pull people towards me.

My daughters were distraught and – understandably – angry. They were very upset about Maggie's death themselves, and to have to live with their father out of the picture too would have landed them in the same predicament as me. I was stunned and ashamed that I'd even contemplated doing something that would put my daughters through what I'd suffered.

I felt I'd acted selfishly and realised I was at a pivotal point – either I carried on as I was or I made even more of an effort to drag myself out of the hole I was in. I made a pact with myself. 'You're in a desperate state,' I told my reflection in the mirror, 'but whatever happens you'll never contemplate – and act on – killing yourself again.'

I'd hit rock bottom. For months I'd been taking one step forward and two steps back, until I'd gone so far back that I'd done something desperate. My self-esteem was in tatters, but acknowledging that fact by shocking myself with my own behaviour was enough to pull me back from the brink of total despair.

I began to get better. It didn't happen overnight, and there were still many dark days for me to face. But gradually, subtly, over the coming months I noticed that I was now beginning to take two steps forward and only one back. When you're coping with depression, it's only when the good days start outnumbering the bad days, and when the bad days are less severe, that you know you're on the road to recovery. For a long time, the bad days had overshadowed the good. But by August 2004, I could feel the balance starting to shift a little. I'll never forget the moment when I realised I'd had two reasonably good days in a row. It was enough to make me hang on a little longer.

CHAPTER 8

THE LIVES OF OTHERS

I began to engage with the world again and do the things I enjoyed. I didn't always want to, but I found that forcing myself out of the house was always a good thing in the end. I began sailing with friends at the weekend; I also dusted off my irons and got back on the golf course. It did me the world of good being on the greens, breathing the fresh air and appreciating nature once more – and on one occasion, it led me to saving another life.

It was a golf day, but I was pretty low and after an early morning patrol I had nearly decided to give my game a miss and go home for a bit. But deep down I knew I'd thank myself later if I just teed up and got on with it. So that's what I did.

Driving back from the game, I went back up to the Head

for another patrol along the cliff edge. I scanned the area with my binoculars and was pleased to observe that all seemed well. Suddenly, I heard the distant roar of an engine and looked around to see a car hurtling down the road. Before long there was sound of rubber screeching into the car park. From my position up on the hill, I saw a figure jump out of the car, slam the door and begin to run up the hill towards the cliff edge.

I soon realised it was a young man, and it was obvious what he was planning to do. In a flash, adrenaline was coursing through my veins. From the direction he was heading in I could guess roughly which point he was aiming to jump from, and I calculated that I might be able to head him off before he got there.

I legged it along the edge like a madman and exhaustedly managed to grab him about 15 ft from where he would have met his end.

He was a stocky young guy and could have floored me in a second if he'd wanted to, but I think he was so shocked that a stranger had pounced on him that he just stood there for a second and wondered what the hell was happening.

'Where on earth do you think you're going, my lad?' I asked as I held him.

'I'm going over there,' he replied, pointing at the edge.

'Oh no you're not!' I said firmly. There was no time for a gently-gently approach this time. I felt that this guy might go for it again at any moment.

'You're not going to stop me!' he shouted, as if preparing to run again.

'I am, or at least I'm going to do my very best to,' I said with conviction. 'I'm between you and this cliff and you've got to get past me to get over there. Now just stop for a second and listen.'

I was desperate to buy myself some time. I hadn't used such a forceful approach before, but on this occasion it felt right. Once again, I wasn't sure where the words were coming from, or what was causing me to act as I did.

'Listen, if you're so determined to kill yourself, you're going to come back in a few minutes and do it anyway, so why not give me five minutes of your time and then make your mind up? Just five minutes…'

The wind picked up for a second, then died down again. We stared at each other, neither of us moving. He didn't say a word, which I took as a cue to continue.

He listened while I explained why I had stopped him, what I was doing up there and how my life was without Maggie.

'Well that knocks my story into a cocked hat, doesn't it?' he exclaimed once I'd finished.

'I don't know,' I laughed. 'What is your story?' Now it was my turn to listen.

He had always had a bad relationship with his father. For years he'd dominated and controlled everything in this boy's life, and now he was studying to go to university and had met a wonderful girl. The problem was that his dad didn't approve and was trying to stop him seeing her.

'He keeps telling me I'm wasting my life on a woman,' said the boy with a look of total despair on his face. I could tell that a lifetime's worth of pain lay behind his words. The rows between him and his dad about this girl and other things sounded horrendous, and from the way he spoke it was obvious that, from an early age, the poor lad's confidence had been snatched away systematically by a very domineering man. To cap it all, his girlfriend had just left him because she couldn't endure the hassle from the father any more. By the time he'd finished his story he was completely beside himself. He couldn't take it any more. It was that simple. That was why he was here.

'So now you know why I want to go,' he finished saying. 'And, listening to your story, I'm surprised you don't want to go yourself!'

'I did,' I replied, 'but I'm glad I didn't follow through.'

Again, a short silence fell between us.

'Do you love your girlfriend?' I asked him.

'I love her more than anything in the world,' he said, crying.

'Well, you've got to be strong. You've got to stand up and tell your father how much you love her, and you must tell your girlfriend too. And once you've told your girlfriend you *both* need to talk to your father. You must lay it on the line to him – make it clear that, no matter what he says or does, you and her are going to be an item. Who knows, you may be together for a year or so, or you might be together forever. Either way, you've got to live for now and make a stand against your father. Only that way will you be able to move on and be your own person. You mustn't let him interfere with your happiness. You're not here because you really want to die, but because you're being held back from *living*. You can move on – this is your chance to think about things and make a stand.'

I took a breath – it had been quite a monologue! By the time I'd finished he was looking at me as if I'd just revealed the secrets of the universe, when all I'd done was speak a little common sense. We walked back to the car, and I cannot describe my sense of relief at saving this young lad. He was only around 18 years old – he had hardly lived – and the idea that he might have ended his life when he had a long life in front of him broke my heart. I was very moved by his story, and even more moved by his gratitude to me. It was even him who suggested we go for a drink.

'Nobody has listened to me like this before,' he said once we were sitting in the pub.

'Well, maybe you haven't given anyone the chance to.'

'You're right,' he shrugged. 'Every time my dad starts, I start ranting too. I've become very volatile and defensive over the years.'

'Well, give your dad a chance to listen, but listen to him too,' I said. 'It takes two to tango, remember.'

He nodded meaningfully. It was wonderful to see the

change in him. When I'd met him, he'd been knotted up with agitation and angst. Now he was completely chilled out.

'What on earth was I thinking?' he said when we got back to the car. 'I don't want to kill myself, so why was I up there?'

I told him it was merely a moment of madness and that he should just look back on it as his lucky day. 'Now go home, count your blessings, and get on with your life.'

'You saved my life,' he said, 'and I can't thank you enough.' I didn't need thanks. Seeing him drive away determined to put things right was enough for me.

I received a phone call from him a couple of days later. He'd made up with his girlfriend and they were just building up the courage to speak to – not shout at – his dad. I told him to make sure he did that and said goodbye.

He is the only person I've saved who has gone public about it – he appeared in a national newspaper article a few years back, and from then on we kept in touch from time to time. Last year I spoke to him and learned that he'd finished university, and that his relationship with his dad was improving – although still a work in progress! The best news was that he was engaged to be married to the girl he still loved more than anything in the world.

I'm very glad I decided to play golf that day.

*   *   *

I'd been shocked at how young that boy was when I saved him. Up until then, I'd only dealt with people with many more years behind them and much more emotional baggage. It came as even more of a shock that my next encounter with a potential jumper was, once again, a young boy.

It was very early one morning. I'd just walked over the brow of the hill when I spotted the lad. He was standing on a flat ledge only a few feet away from Maggie's cross. He was on the edge of a sheer 550 ft drop, and his body language told me he was ready to jump. He looked like a man about to parachute from an aeroplane. His knees were bent, his fists were clenched by his side and, worst of all, his toes were sticking out over the cliff edge. His face was set with a look of utter determination and focus.

My heart skipped a beat. I knew I only had seconds to make an impression on him. If I got it wrong, he'd be gone.

Calling out to someone so close to the edge of a cliff is dangerous at the best of times – you can startle them and potentially make them fall by accident if they turn to see who is calling. But I had no choice. I wasn't close enough to appeal to him in gentle and sensitive tone, nor could I get to him quickly enough to stop him physically. I couldn't risk him jumping while I ran towards him, so I took a chance.

'STOP! NOW!' I called out.

Luckily, he froze to the spot. I carried on talking as I walked towards him.

'Look, I don't know what the problem is but please, *please* let me speak to you. The position you're in means there's nothing I can do to stop you going, but just give me one chance. Please, hear me out!'

In truth, I would have tried to grab him, even if it meant that I might go with him. I'd done it before and I've done it since. But just then, all I wanted was his trust.

Very, very slowly, I walked up and stood next to him at the edge. I could see that he was only around 17.

'What's this all about?' I asked. 'Are you from Eastbourne?'

'No, Cheshire.'

'Well, what are you doing here?'

He replied without hesitation. 'I'm a failure, a complete failure.'

'How can you be a *complete* failure?' I asked. 'Nobody's a *complete* failure. You're not even old enough to be a failure – what on earth are you failing at?'

'College,' he replied. 'That's what.'

'Who says so?' I challenged him.

It turned out that one of his tutors had told him that if he failed at college, he wouldn't succeed in life. All his life, the boy had felt like a failure. He felt like he'd always been put down and dismissed. The tutor's recent comments were the straw that broke the camel's back. Because he wasn't doing well in education, the boy felt that his life would fail as his tutor predicted. Therefore there was no point in living any longer. He'd driven down from Cheshire overnight so he would arrive at Beachy Head by morning. On arriving, he sat in the car for a while, and decided it was time to go over the edge once and for all.

The boy had hardly moved an inch. He was perilously close to falling to his death. I had to say something – and fast.

'Well, all I can tell you is that you're absolutely not a failure. The first thing you have to do in life is succeed as a person. GCSEs, A-Levels and other qualifications have nothing to do with success as a human being. I haven't got a qualification to my name but I make a very good living, and I was married and very happy. Unfortunately, my wife went the way you're about to go.'

I hoped that what I was saying was starting to sink in. 'Have you got a family?' I asked. He did – mum, dad, sister and brother. 'Well, do they think you're a failure?'

'I think they do…' he replied meekly.

'Have they told you that?'

'No, I just feel it and now my tutor's just told me I am.'

'Well, I think you ought to chat to your family about it – don't you? You love your sister, right?'

He nodded.

'Well she ain't gonna like you if you do this,' I continued. 'She's gonna hate you, because it's very easy to hate someone who does this. No one deserves to be put through such a thing. Do you think she deserves that?'

The boy looked glum, but I could tell I was getting through. It was time to try and get him away from that edge.

'Please step back just a few feet so we can at least talk properly,' I urged him.

He shuffled onto a flat ledge a few feet back and we sat down together.

'Look,' I said, putting my arm around him, 'what you're thinking of doing is a desperate measure and I really think that if you come along with me now we can try to sort this out. If you can't talk to your family how about you feel, then give me a chance to tell them.'

The boy agreed to let me call his dad, who was over the moon to hear his son was OK and totally shocked to discover that he was in Eastbourne. The Cheshire police had already been called, so because it was already a police matter I had to inform the Eastbourne police of our whereabouts. They met us at the Beachy Head pub and were wonderfully kind to the boy. They told him he wasn't in any trouble at all and explained that they were only there to return him safely to his parents.

As we shook hands and said goodbye, I could see tears forming in the boy's eyes. 'Thanks so much,' he said earnestly. 'I just want to go home and have a good life.'

Off he went. As for having a good life, his sister called me six months later with some wonderful news. The boy was doing well at college and his frame of mind was completely different. The family had taken time to have long chats about all of his worries and problems and it really did turn out to be a case of a problem shared being a problem halved – or in this case, solved. That phone call gave me a real boost. I'm really meant to be doing this, I thought. It felt like fate had brought me to Beachy Head to save as many lives as possible.

★   ★   ★

I don't class myself as a hero. I didn't then, and I don't now. Soldiers are heroes – they go off and fight for their countries. Firemen are heroes – they run into blazing houses. But I don't like the word when it is applied to me. As far as I'm concerned, I'm just an ordinary bloke who cares passionately about life and about people not being subjected to what I've been through. In light of this, it came as a bit of shock when I opened the post one morning in August 2004 to discover that the Humane Society were writing to tell me I'd been given the Millennium Award for bravery. It was a complete surprise and I could hardly believe it. It turned out that the Eastbourne police had nominated me on the back of my first ever save – the girl whom I'd rugby tackled and visited in hospital. Naturally, I was flattered, but really didn't feel worthy of such an accolade. My view was that I'd only done what anybody would have tried to do.

I almost turned the award down. Contrary to what some might say, I never actively sought publicity in order to promote myself during my time at Beachy Head. It was around this time that the media got wind of my patrols and began to get in touch with me. I was very wary of any publicity, though, and found the award a bit daunting. My family tried to convince me I should accept it. They argued that I had saved a life, after all, and that it was an act of bravery in many people's eyes. I could understand this point, of course, but it wasn't enough to convince me. I needed a better reason. Someone suggested that the award might help me in my quest for 24-hour patrols at Beachy Head. It was a national award, they argued, and accepting it would give me a platform from which to raise awareness about suicide up at Beachy Head. It would give me a profile that may help me when lobbying the council. Put simply, the award would give me a voice.

They were all valid points. Indeed, I was desperate to find a way of approaching the council from a strong position, and the award certainly couldn't do any harm. So, after much umming and ahhing, I decided to accept.

The local papers announced that I was to receive the award, and the nationals soon picked up on it too. Before I knew it I was receiving one phone call after another from members of the media asking for comments, interviews and filming opportunities – and it was pretty overwhelming at first! Oh shit, I thought, what on earth have I got myself into? What have I started? The truth is, I wasn't sure. I wasn't looking for publicity for me. I was looking for publicity for Beachy Head and its problems.

All I knew was that now I'd begun, there was no turning back. Consequently, I always tried to keep in mind that this new-found publicity could be just what I needed to help achieve my goals. Without that in mind, it would have been very tempting to turn my phone off for good!

The award ceremony was held at Eastbourne Town Hall. The Mayoress and the Chief Inspector of Eastbourne Police presented me with the certificate and the BBC came along to film it. From that moment on the press coverage went a bit mad, and it was a perfect opportunity to drum into the public how strongly I felt that Beachy Head needed cover – and that I felt the matter was the responsibility of the Eastbourne Council. In 12 months, 34 people had died up at Beachy Head. I reasoned that if 34 people had died at a road junction it would be classed as an accident black spot and that many thousands of pounds would have been spent on rebuilding the junction to make it safe. But even though Beachy Head is part of the Borough of Eastbourne, the council denied it was their responsibility to provide 24-hour cover up there.

I found this hard to swallow. In my view, the fact that the council charge for parking at Beachy Head, that they even charge film and television companies to film up there and they collect fines from people who flout those rules, means that it should also be their responsibility to try to prevent people dying. It is the least they could do. If looking after the people who visit it isn't part of looking after Beachy Head, then something is very wrong.

I plugged my cause wherever I could. The media were suddenly very interested in the window cleaner from

Eastbourne who was lobbying the council, and the calls kept coming. The BBC World Service interviewed me, *Reader's Digest* featured me in their magazine, *The Trisha Goddard Show* wanted me on along with countless other news and current affairs programmes. Later on, I would go on *This Morning*.

Being thrust into the limelight was a strange experience, but I soon began to feel comfortable talking to people who seemed genuinely interested in my cause. I was surprised but pleased by all the hype because I really thought it would make a difference. Sad to say, as far as Eastbourne Council were concerned, it made none.

One (very comforting) result of all the press coverage was the letters I received from people who had been affected by my story. Correspondence poured in from all over the world (thanks to *Reader's Digest*, among other international publications). I received many heart-rending letters and emails from America, Australia, South Africa and even Japan, all of them touchingly supportive. Some people were simply moved by my plight and wrote the kindest words of encouragement; others had lost loved ones to suicide and wanted to share their experiences and tell me that my story had helped give them strength. Quite a few of the stories I received were truly moving, some were horrific – hearing what other people had been through often made my problems seem rather insignificant by comparison.

I appeared on John Peel's *Home Truths* on Radio 4, and

once again it prompted a huge response from listeners. It was almost like fan mail, but with a difference – I was hearing from people who had been helped and inspired by my story, but their stories and words of encouragement were helping me too. As each day went by, I found my resolve to keep doing what I was doing growing ever stronger.

Inevitably, I suppose, there came a time when I began to attract rather more negative comments too. I was accused of self-promotion. I was accused of trying to become a celebrity. I was accused of drawing attention to Beachy Head and potentially attracting more suicidal people to the area. I was even accused of making money out of my wife's death. All of these accusations were immensely hurtful. The comments didn't come from the media, but from certain people who were close to me and in letters printed in papers.

Suddenly, I realised that there were some people who actually didn't like me for what I was doing. The idea that I was courting fame was simply absurd – much of the time I was still very low, and I certainly didn't want to be walking on any red carpets. I wanted 24-hour cover for a suicide spot – that was all. During the four years I patrolled up at Beachy Head, figures for deaths varied hugely year on year. Looking at the numbers, it's simply impossible to see any correlation between me and suicide rates. I was amazed that people seriously felt my media presence and patrolling was making the situation worse.

Being accused of profiting from my activities was the most

insulting thing I had to endure. I wasn't making a penny out of my work. Any fees that I received from interviews were put in a special bank account. It was special because it was being set aside for an idea I had first come up with that August. I'd decided to start a charity and I wanted to call it the Maggie Lane Trust. I wanted to raise money to help fund patrols at Beachy Head and to help those who were suicidal and their families and loved ones. But I soon learned that you can't set up a charity overnight, so for the time being the money was put away safely until the right moment came. It would be some time before the charity became official, although even in those early days I was able to give money to the chaplains. But I'm getting ahead of myself...

*   *   *

It was October 2004 and Maggie's birthday had come around. Media frenzy or no media frenzy, I'd still been patrolling every day, still trying to come to terms with Maggie's death, and I'd been dreading the day when I would be celebrating my wife's entry into the world, but this time without her. Now I was alone. Throughout September, I found myself thinking more and more about my dear, departed wife. The week leading up to her birthday was strange in two ways. Firstly, three teenagers died up at Beachy Head during that period. While this was thoroughly depressing, it was also very unusual – it was rare that so many deaths happened in such a short space of time and very disturbing that the victims were all youngsters. Secondly, just before the day I was so dreading, I received a phone call from Jules, the spiritualist I had been seeing.

'What's going on at Beachy Head?' she asked. I assumed she knew about the boys, but she didn't. 'Maggie's told me we have to sort Beachy Head out,' she continued, 'so I wondered if anything strange has been going on up there.'

Slightly confused, I told her about the boys and also mentioned that a paedophile had committed suicide the week before. He was about to be tried for his crimes, but had obviously been unable to face the courts.

'Maybe that's the problem Maggie's talking about,' Jules said, mysteriously. 'I need to come by Beachy Head and sort it out.' I told Jules about Maggie's approaching birthday and we decided to go up to the Head together on the day. So now I wouldn't be alone after all…

The day came. I bought a huge bouquet of flowers, and after visiting Maggie's grave, I picked Jules up. We drove to the car park I always parked in and got out.

Immediately, Jules pointed to a certain place at the cliff edge. 'Did the paedophile die at that point?' she asked.

'Yes,' I told her, amazed.

'I can see him up there now,' she said, her face concentrated and serious. 'He has a troubled soul. He has problems and hasn't crossed over properly to the other side. He's trying to cause havoc up there. He's looking for vulnerable people to pull over the edge. It seems that he's succeeding, too. *Think about those three boys.*' Jules' words sent a shiver down my spine. I said nothing, and wondered how she would proceed from here.

First, we went up to Maggie's cross. I was carrying the bouquet and some other flowers – whenever I visited Maggie's grave, I always changed her flowers and took the used ones up to Beachy Head with me so that I could throw them over the cliff by her cross. Unusually for Beachy Head, it was completely windless that day. But as I threw the flowers over, a wind that seemed to come from nowhere took them and blew them right over my head and on to the grass behind me. I looked at Jules in amazement.

'Maggie doesn't want those today,' she said, smiling at me. 'It's her birthday! Throw the bouquet over for her!'

The air was windless again. I threw the bouquet over the edge, but it didn't fall far. Instead, the wind whipped up again and pinned it to the cliff face. There was nothing to support or trap it – it just stayed there, as if clinging to the cliff. I was gobsmacked, and could hardly believe my eyes.

'Don't worry,' said Jules, still smiling. 'Just go with the flow.'

I relaxed and looked back at the bouquet. It was still there. Jules suggested we walked up to the spot where the paedophile, or at least the paedophile's troubled soul, was lurking. She had work to do, and on my late wife's instruction too, so we moved away from Maggie's spot. As we walked, I wondered what would happen to Maggie's bouquet of flowers while we were gone.

As we climbed, the wind flared up again. With every step we took, it got stronger and stronger. By the time we got there, both of us were leaning into it. I couldn't fathom where such a wind had suddenly come from.

'He's worried,' Jules said, taking my hand. 'He's resisting, but don't worry. Keep hold of me and keep going.'

We got as close as we could to where the paedophile's spirit was lurking. Soon the wind was so fierce that we could go no further. Steadying herself, Jules faced the wind and began to speak. It was obvious she was shouting but her words were inaudible to me – the frenzied wind simply whipped them away. It didn't matter, though, for I knew Jules' words were not for my ears but for the tormented soul who was fighting her.

The wind didn't die down; it didn't taper off slowly. It simply stopped. One second, it felt like a full-force gale; the next second, nothing. The contrast took my breath away.

'It's all right,' said Jules as she turned to me and breathed out. 'He's crossed over. It's safe now. Let's go and say goodbye to Maggie.'

I nodded, stunned but calm. I felt safe with Jules.

Back at Maggie's cross, I went to lean over and check on the bouquet of flowers, but Jules got in my way.

'Hang on a second,' she said calmly. 'Before you do that, I'm just going to say a few words to the angels.'

I stood back. Jules took a breath and began to speak. As she talked, something truly incredible happened. Suddenly, the flower petals flew from the bouquet, came up the cliff and blew up into the air in front of us before floating over our heads to form a circle in the air. There they remained for a few seconds before moving westwards in an arc and disappearing back over the cliff edge a little further along from where we stood. It was stunning – magical, beautiful – and as the petals danced in the air I could do nothing but stand there in awe, my mouth agape and my entire body covered in goose bumps.

The whole experience completely took my breath away. What I'd seen was no accident or freak wind. It was the work of something else. It was the work of Maggie's spirit and to me it was her way of telling me all was well with her – her way of reaching out and offering me comfort. That extraordinary moment was the first time I gained real insight into the world that Jules was so connected to, and it gave me a deep feeling of well-being.

Up until that day, I'd always been sceptical about the possibility of spirits and life beyond the grave, but I could not dismiss what I had just witnessed. What I saw was as true as night following day and from then on I knew there had to be something more to this world than I'd previously thought possible.

★   ★   ★

A few months later, I would have another spiritual encounter up at the edge, but this time it wasn't nearly so uplifting. In fact, I nearly lost my life.

Once again I was up at Maggie's cross during a patrol. It was around 4 am and semi-dark. The air was damp, and Beachy Head had a very eerie feel about it that morning. As I stood at the edge, I was suddenly overcome by a terrible sense of foreboding. Something felt bad, yet I couldn't quite put my finger on what was wrong, so I tried to ignore my instincts and get on with things.

It might sound odd to anyone who has not visited a grave or a cross of a loved one, but once Maggie had died I never stopped talking to her when I visited the places that marked her memory. As I stood at her cross, I would often say, 'Hello, darling' and tell her my thoughts, always hoping she would hear my words. This morning was no different. Even though I had a very uneasy feeling as I approached her cross, I still spoke to her.

'Good morning, darling,' I said as I stepped forward cautiously. 'How are you today?'

Some might think 'How are you?' is a pretty strange question to ask a dead person, but that didn't stop me! As I moved forward I became even more uncomfortable and had a feeling that someone was near me, so I looked around. Nobody. I moved a little closer.

As I took my final step towards the cross I felt a sudden shove in my back and was pushed very firmly forwards. It certainly wasn't the wind – this was a sudden pressure and I could feel it getting stronger. Something was trying to push me over the edge.

A feeling of complete terror came over me. In an instant, I pushed back and turned to run. I was frightened to death! I was brought up to look after myself fearlessly, and even though I'm a small man I've never been frightened of anybody. This was different, though. I was being pushed by someone, or *something*, that I couldn't even see! I ran like the clappers all the way back to the car, and my panic didn't begin to subside until I was safely back in central Eastbourne.

Beachy Head is a spiritual place. They say that witchcraft goes on up there, and many spiritualists will tell you that both good and bad spirits lurk around those cliffs. I've seen spiritualists performing rituals up on the hill in an effort to keep bad spirits at bay, and my experience that morning only served to warn me that the spirit world is something to treat with reverence. I could well have fallen farther that morning and from then on I was much more cautious when standing alone at the edge.

Scared as I'd been, I still went back up the next morning and continued my patrols. Whether it was the media, my job, my unhappiness – or even bad spirits! – my work came first, and if I wasn't up there for three patrols a day then I wasn't the man the newspapers were saying I was.

CHAPTER 9

DOWN AND
NEARLY OUT

I was walking along Terminus Road in Eastbourne one day when I noticed a man heading my way. He was young and staring at me intensely. Immediately, I became a little nervous. As quick as a flash he came right up to me and grabbed me. From his movements I thought he was about to head butt me, so I prepared to defend myself. But he was on me in a flash – though not with a head butt. Just as I was recoiling from him, he placed a kiss in the middle of my forehead.

'What was that for?' I exclaimed, relieved yet stunned.

'You don't know me, but I know you,' he replied. 'I've heard about you and I know what you've done.'

I was intrigued to find out why he had stopped me for a kiss, so I waited to hear what he had to say for himself.

'You saved my mum's life up at Beachy Head,' he continued, 'and I'm so glad you're here now so that I can thank you.'

Immediately, I felt elated. It's always wonderful when someone confirms that you've made a difference. I asked him how his mum was, but before he answered his face became a little sad.

'I'm afraid she died about six weeks after you saved her,' he said. Oh my God, I thought, She went back a second time and jumped. My joy gave way to a sense of utter failure. I was lost for words for a second. Why is he thanking me? I wondered. Seconds later I received my answer.

'Before you say anything,' continued the lad, 'she didn't die at Beachy Head. She died of cancer. You're probably wondering why I'm thanking you, since she died anyway, but what you did for us is still incredible. You gave us six extra weeks of our mother's life. We were able to say goodbye. If she had gone over at Beachy Head, she'd have cheated us of that time and things would have been so different. I want to thank you from the bottom of my heart.'

I was truly taken aback at the humanity and strength of this man. Even though he'd lost his mum, he still had room in his heart to brush aside that pain for a few moments and take the time to thank me. I remembered his mum very well now he had told me his story and after we'd exchanged a few more words we wished each other the best of luck before going our separate ways.

Like thousands of people who lose loved ones to suicide each year, I did not have the chance to say goodbye to Maggie and not having that chance made my grief for her so much harder to work through. There were so many unsaid things and so many unanswered questions; trying to live with what had happened was often pure agony. To think that I'd spared one family that pain and given them a chance to achieve closure made me feel great. I was lucky to have encountered this man – not least because I learned a new lesson that would prove invaluable in my work up at Beachy Head.

Up until now, whenever I'd confronted someone at the cliff edge who had a terminal illness, I found it virtually impossible to know what to say to them. After all, it's no good telling someone with six months to live that they have everything to live for. What *do* you say to a terminally ill person, I'd often wonder. Now I had the answer on a plate. I could talk to them about their relatives, plead with them: 'Please don't cheat your loved ones of the chance to say goodbye to you.' I would use that line on numerous subsequent occasions during my life on the edge and I'm pleased to say it worked.

I only have the man from whom I expected a head butt to thank for that.

* * *

Publicly, life was going well. I was saving lives, the media were ever-supportive of my campaign against the council and money was building up in my special account as I prepared for the Maggie Lane Trust to open officially. Privately, though, I was still a mess.

No matter what I did, I still couldn't move on from Maggie and the misery her death had caused me. For a while I'd been getting by on two good days out of three, but by the time the anniversary of Maggie's death came around, my depression was starting to destroy me again. For obvious reasons, the marker of a year gone by was a massive psychological obstacle for me to face, and the more I thought about it, the more I relived the pain of a year previously.

I was in financial trouble too. While Maggie had been ill, we had fallen behind on payments for the house and now she was gone I wasn't able to work enough hours to meet them. Due to a loophole in her life insurance policy, I finally learned that I would not be receiving any money from that and this news was the final straw. I would have to sell our house.

I'd owned the house before I met Maggie, but when she had moved in her female touch had transformed the place. Exactly to Maggie's specifications, we redecorated from top to bottom so that she would be comfortable. We had turned my house into our home and having to sell it was heartbreaking.

Since she'd died, I'd left everything as it was. Our bedroom was like a shrine – all of Maggie's clothes and other belongings were exactly where she had left them, and now I was being forced to move them. But I couldn't take them with me, as I had nowhere to move but in with a friend. It was time to move on, I guess, but as I packed all of her lovely clothes into boxes bound for the charity shop, I didn't feel like I wanted to move on one bit. It took several trips to the charity shop and back before I'd finally got rid of everything she owned, and as I removed each box from the house I felt like I was removing one more piece of Maggie. It was one of the hardest things I've ever had to do. I felt like I was getting rid of my wife and I felt horrible about it.

There was one thing I couldn't get rid of just yet, though: Maggie's wedding outfit. I carefully packed her beautiful white dress, her long blue coat, her delicate white shoes and her handbag into a suitcase. It was the one piece of Maggie I would take with me. By the time I'd moved everything out of our house and made the place spotless for the new owner, the only thing that remained was one of my favourite photographs of Maggie. It stood alone in its frame on the mantelpiece.

Eventually, it was time to leave. The buyer – a woman who was planning on renting the place out – came round to collect the keys. We stood in the living room for a while and I swooned a little as I stared around at the emptiness of the house. So much had changed within a year. I handed the keys over to the woman, walked up to the picture and took it in my hands.

'Come on darling, it's time for us to go,' I said, bursting

into tears. The woman could see the hurt in me and began to cry too. I'll never forget those final moments in our house, and I'll never forget how strange it was to walk out and drive off knowing I would never return.

Moving out didn't help me move on. Not at first. I was living with a friend, and the dreaded anniversary was just around the corner.

When I'd gone up to Beachy Head thinking I was going to kill myself back in 2004, I'd come down and sworn to myself I would never contemplate such a thing again. I'm sad to say, though, that by the time the day of the anniversary came around, I was doing just that. But this time, it was more than a drunken impulse. I'd been planning it for around a month. On the anniversary of Maggie's death I was planning to bring about my own.

The day came. My family were naturally worried about how I would fare on such a painfully significant occasion, and they had asked me to stay in touch so they knew that I was OK. Well, there was no way I was going to keep in contact with anybody. I'd decided I was going to retrace Maggie's steps from that fateful day, and then end my day in the way that she had. I was going to copy her.

First of all, I began driving to the rope company she had been working for. On the drive there, I stopped off for a bacon sandwich and a cup of tea at my brother's kiosk on the A22. We chatted away and, knowing what I was about to do, I made an effort to be cheery in case my family called him later on. I knew I wasn't going to respond, so I wanted him to tell them he'd seen me and that I was fine. As far as he was concerned, I was merely on my way to Maggie's last workplace to have a bit of a chat with the people there. We said goodbye and I drove on.

'Do you mind if I come in?' I said to the boss when I arrived at the rope company. 'This may seem strange but I need to relive Maggie's last day and trace all of her movements.'

He did think it was a little odd, but graciously granted me my wish. I was introduced to someone who'd been around on Maggie's last day, and they told me about her behaviour on that first (remember, she was just starting there) and final morning. I was told that Maggie had seemed strange from the moment she turned up – it was as if she were on a different planet. She had seemed confused, fumbled with the coffee machine and got lost looking for the toilets. True, it was her first day, and because they liked her they had wanted to give her the benefit of the doubt, yet her odd behaviour was already making them wonder how useful she would be as an employee.

I saw the desk where Maggie had sat. I saw the rope-making area that she had run a few errands to. I looked at the rope. I don't know quite where the impulse came from, but I asked the boss if I could have some.

'How much do you need?' he asked.

'Oh, about 100 ft,' I said casually.

'Why do you want it?'

'That's my business.' I answered defensively. The truth was that I wasn't quite sure what I wanted it for. I suppose I was in a pretty deranged state (as anyone might be when planning to commit suicide). I had a vague idea that I might use the rope up at Beachy Head in some way. But, looking back, I can see that my actions and words were downright bizarre.

Since it was the anniversary of Maggie's death, the boss was highly suspicious. Clearly, he thought I was going to hang myself. It didn't matter what I said, the answer was a resolute 'No way.'

I left the rope company and drove along the route I'd guessed Maggie must have taken when she left. She'd told me she was going to meet a friend, so I headed towards the friend's house. I had a strange sense of acting out some weird scenario – as if I was pretending to be Maggie in order to try and get close to her again. I was feeling irrational and strange, but Maggie must have been in a comparable state of mind herself on the same day the previous year.

On the way I stopped off at B&Q. I had no problem buying 100 ft of rope there. Next, I pulled up outside the friend's house and just sat in the car for a while. This was where Maggie had made her last phone call to me, I thought to myself. This was where she'd last said 'I love you.' This was the point from which she'd set off to Beachy Head. Now it was my turn to do the same.

Snow was falling thick and fast. As I drove it got heavier and before long I had to stop. It was as if the elements were against me. Someone doesn't want me to be up at Beachy Head today, I thought. Little did I care. I got out of the car, took the rope, a shovel and a wreath of flowers from the boot, and began to walk.

By the time I was halfway up the hill, I was walking in a blizzard. It didn't matter; I knew where I was going. I arrived at Maggie's spot. The only trouble was that it was buried under 4 feet of snow! A drift had built up, so I could hardly tell where the cliff edge was. Nevertheless, I began to dig like a man possessed, creating a tunnel to get to the cross. My mind was in such disarray that for a time it didn't occur to me that I could be digging my way towards thin air and death. I wanted to die, but not until I'd found what I was looking for. Once I had Maggie's cross in my hand, I'd be ready to join her. Somehow, it mattered more than anything that I had the cross before I went.

After ten minutes of frantic digging, I'd created a massive tunnel. The cross was nowhere to be seen, though. Then, suddenly, I began to recognise the terrain I was digging over and knew I was getting very close. I also knew I was near the edge. If I slipped now, I would fall. It was time to use the rope. I tied it to a couple of poles nearby and wrapped it around my waist.

I won't fall now, I thought. And then I laughed. If I'm up here to die, I thought, why have I tied a rope around my waist? In that moment of laughter it struck me that, once again, my mind had been playing tricks on itself again. I'd been convincing myself I wanted to do something, but it turned out that I wanted to do the opposite. I didn't want to die – I wanted to pay my respects to Maggie and live!

It amazes me how, in the space of a moment, a person can switch from being hell-bent on ending their life to realising it's the last thing they want. But it is possible, as I've learned a couple of times. In my case, my mind had become so fragile from grief and depression that some of the time I simply didn't know if I was coming or going. The intensity of emotion that Maggie's anniversary provoked had led me to behave in an extreme way – I'd temporarily lost control and deluded myself into thinking death was the answer to my problems. It had appealed as an escape, an easy way out.

In that moment of clarity, I realised just how daft I must have looked. I was up on Beachy Head in a blizzard, shovel in hand, rope round my waist and all the while carrying a wreath! I laughed some more, and it occurred to me that Maggie's spirit may well have made sure there was all that snow for me to get through. Having to dig for so long gave me time to realise just what I was doing.

'You crafty cow,' I said out loud as I laid the wreath by Maggie's cross. 'You didn't want me to die up here – you know I should be saving others, not killing myself! I love you, sweetheart!'

★   ★   ★

My actions that day meant one thing: I still wasn't well. I still missed Maggie like crazy and I was still prone to taking desperate measures to deal with my problems. Once again, I resolved to try harder to get better. However, I still didn't know where to start. All I knew was that being close to Maggie would bring me comfort. And the only way I could be near her was through spiritual contact. Jules had become a good friend by now, however, and she felt that our friendship could interfere with her ability to make contact with Maggie. A friend recommended somebody else to me.

Jane's house was a beautiful haven of tranquillity surrounded by well-kept lawns and peaceful ponds. As soon as she opened her front door to me, I felt at ease. We went into her room upstairs and I sat down.

Jane worked differently to Jules: her technique was to write down what the spirits told her. She told me to relax, took my hand and closed her eyes. After a short time she began to write and to my amazement she was telling me things about myself that she had no way of knowing. She talked about my family, my past actions, experiences I had been through. Then she began to talk about Maggie.

Maggie was at peace. To hear this was an indescribable relief; I could feel the emotion welling up inside me. My breathing slowed and I began to feel even calmer. She had been through so much pain, but she was going through the healing process now. There was no need for me to worry, Maggie was becoming at one with herself again.

And then Jane told me something incredible: 'Maggie's coming to join us,' she said. 'Please don't be frightened. She's already in the room and she's with me at the moment. I want you to close your eyes, sit back and tell me what you feel...' This could be it, I thought. This could be my moment with Maggie. I closed my eyes and waited.

'All right,' said Jane very gently. 'She's coming over to you now.'

Suddenly, my left hand turned freezing cold. It was absolutely icy. At the same time, an intense wave of warmth spread through the rest of my body. I could feel all my negative, anxious thoughts draining from me and within a few moments I was in such a state of peace that it was almost overwhelming.

'Maggie's sitting beside you to the left,' said Jane soothingly. 'How do you feel?'

I told her how cold my left hand was.

'Relax,' she replied. 'Maggie's just giving you some healing.'

Just as suddenly as my hand had turned cold, it became boiling hot. I was warm all over and more at peace than I'd been in a very long time. The sense of release was staggering.

Slowly, beautifully, the warmth began to fade.

'You can open your eyes,' said Jane. 'There are other spirits around but Maggie has left the room for now.'

I opened my eyes. It was like waking from a wonderful sleep. This was the first time I had felt Maggie's spirit touching me, and it was profoundly moving. I'd been in her presence, I knew it and I was as high as a kite. My elation was such that I could have jumped for joy, but looking at my watch I realised there was no time to jump for anything. In only 15 minutes I had to be up on Beachy Head for a TV interview and I was 10 miles away!

I thanked Jane profusely and dashed out to my car, explaining why I had to rush off. As I got into the car I was overcome by a very powerful smell – Maggie's perfume. The scent filled the car and I took a deep breath. I was calm again for a few moments.

'You're here, aren't you Maggie?' I said to the passenger seat. 'Now, get me to Beachy Head!'

As I drove through Eastbourne, I could hardly believe what was happening. Every light was green, every roundabout was clear and every junction was empty of other cars. Before I knew it I was pulling into Beachy Head car park, and I even had a minute to spare before my interview. I'd driven 10 miles through a built-up area in only 14 minutes.

'Thank you, sweetheart,' I exclaimed and turned the engine off. The smell of Maggie's perfume had been with me all the way, but now it vanished. Maggie had gone. I didn't feel sad – simply grateful for everything I'd experienced that morning.

Maggie had made contact and she'd helped me get to Beachy Head in time. She'd also helped me to feel a little more alive again.

Looking back, I think Maggie was preparing me to move on. Little did I know that my life was about to begin again, and that my new beginning was just around the corner.

CHAPTER 10

LIGHT AND LOVE
AT THE END OF
THE TUNNEL

Gradually, I started to come out of my shell. Instead of sitting at home, drinking alone, I began to go out every now and then. I was still on my own, but at least I was out. Granted, I'd still get absolutely plastered in the corner of whatever pub or club I was in, and I'd still be as miserable as sin. But at least I wasn't doing it in my front room. It was progress – of sorts.

One pub I frequented, the Prince Albert, had a different band on every week and I began going there for the music. One Friday night, I happened to be there with a woman who had accompanied me when I went on the *Trisha* show. She was just a friend – at that stage even thinking about other women made me feel guilty. If I caught someone's eye I would feel like I was betraying my late wife. Most of the time, there wasn't even anyone whose eye I wanted to catch; I was resolute that nobody could compare with my Maggie. Well, that night that I was proved wrong.

My friend and I were standing at the bar and, much to my embarrassment, she was boasting loudly that we'd both been on the *Trisha* show. I can't stand showing off and every time she spoke it made me cringe. I hardly knew where to look.

Right by me was a woman I had seen a few times previously. I'd smiled at her once or twice, and I certainly did fancy her. But each time I saw her I felt too guilty about Maggie to be able to say hello. Instead, I averted my eyes. Tricky to do when that person is standing next to you, though!

'Don't worry,' she said, nodding towards my boastful friend, 'we all know where she's coming from. I know you're not like that.'

I smiled. My embarrassment about the bragging must have been pretty obvious, then.

'Take no notice,' she continued. 'Nobody else is!'

I was pretty taken aback that this beautiful woman had seen how uncomfortable I was and had taken the trouble to approach me about it. There was no way I could avoid talking to her this time. Before, I'd only seen her from across the room. Now, close up, she was even more attractive than I'd previously thought. What's more, I felt pretty at ease with her, all things considered. I was a little nervous, but comfortable enough to offer her a drink.

'Only if I can buy you one back,' she said, smiling. 'I don't accept drinks from men who are only after one thing.'

I laughed and told her I'm wasn't that kind of bloke, but that I'd take on board what she was saying. I told her if she felt that way she could buy the drinks first.

'You sod,' she said, her smile broadening. We laughed a little together. We were enjoying winding each other up a bit. This was my kind of woman!

'I'm Keith, by the way.'

'Val,' she said.

We hit it off immediately. As we talked I became mesmerised by her company. I was very relaxed – more relaxed than I'd felt with anyone in a long, long time. I quickly realised I was falling for her hook, line and sinker. But I had to check myself. I didn't want to rush. I didn't want to fall too hard. I wanted to take my time. As it turned out, I didn't have to worry too much – Val was separated, but she had been seeing someone and he was due to arrive at the pub any minute!

'Got to go now,' she said as he stepped through the pub door. But before she slipped away, she gave me her number. 'I've got a villa in Spain. If you ever want to get away from all this media stuff and have a break, come and see me. There's plenty of bedrooms. I'll be there for the next three weeks...'

I was stunned. I'd only just met this woman, and already she'd offered me a room in a villa so I could take a break from the media — and a break was just what I needed right then. Plus, boyfriend or no boyfriend, I *really* liked this woman. As we had chatted at the bar, I'd told myself not to rush. Now I was standing alone again, rushing suddenly seemed a lot more appealing. It wasn't like I had much to lose.

It was time to book a flight to Spain.

★   ★   ★

I'm not normally scared of flying, but I was nervous on that flight. *Very* nervous. What did I think I was doing? I hardly knew this woman, and she had a boyfriend. Still, I couldn't turn the plane around. I'd made my bed — now I'd just have to lie in it.

Val met me at the airport. When I saw her, my jaw dropped. She was wearing a flowing white dress that highlighted a tan she'd acquired and she looked absolutely stunning. I looked at her blonde hair and drank in her warm smile. Wow!

It was like history repeating itself… We chatted and laughed like old friends as we drove through the Spanish mountains towards Torrox, and with every bend in the road I became more comfortable in Val's company. By the time we arrived at her villa in the hills, she had totally disarmed me.

I was giddy as we walked into the villa. I felt simply wonderful. Before she'd come to pick me up, Val had put some champagne on ice. As we drank it on her terrace in the warmth of the sun, I knew I'd fallen for her.

We talked and giggled some more and flirted coyly with each other. I knew what I was feeling and I could tell Val had feelings for me too. There was a serious chemistry between us and, inevitably, it wasn't long before we were in each other's arms making passionate love.

The last few hours had been a whirlwind. I'd gone from wondering what the hell I was doing on a plane to lying in bed with a woman I was quickly falling in love with.

Val told me that her relationship was history. She had let the guy go soon after meeting me. 'I told him I couldn't see him any more,' she said as we lay together. 'The moment I met you I knew I wanted to be with you and that was it.' It felt magical that Val was showing such powerful emotions after such a short space of time, and more amazing still because I felt so strongly about her too.

I pulled her closer. Everything felt so natural with Val. It's hard to describe what a wonderful sense of relief I felt at being suddenly so close to another person again. And this wasn't just any person: she was perfect.

Naturally, however, my thoughts turned to Maggie. While Val was out of the room, I stepped out onto the balcony and looked across the valley. The sky was clear and blue, and in the distance I could see trees perched on mountains that squatted under the sun.

'I'm sorry, darling,' I said out loud to Maggie. 'I'm only human. I'm enjoying myself again. I'm back in the land of the living. I've got feelings and I want to be intimate with someone. I want to love and I want to be loved. I hope you don't mind, in fact I'm sure you don't. I feel that you've guided me here, sweetheart.'

I have often said that I think Maggie hand-picked Val for me. Maggie had made contact with me and guided me that day back in England and I think she was giving me that healing so that I would be ready to accept Val when I met her. In short, Maggie was helping me move on from Maggie.

Knowing Maggie as I did, it would have been just like her to say, 'You're on this planet, I'm not. You've only got one crack at life so, for God's sake, get on with it. You've got a wonderful woman, now enjoy her!'

And that's what I did. I knew what was happening with Val was right. I never doubted it and from that moment on the balcony I never looked back.

We were inseparable from the off. In addition to us both being the same height – about five-foot four – we quickly discovered that we have the same sense of humour and the same zest for life. We found that we both love sport and it wasn't long before I was teaching Val how to play pool and she was teaching me how to enjoy swimming. But more than anything, in that week we discovered that we simply loved each other's company.

I wasn't looking forward to saying goodbye at all. We arrived at the airport and I got out of the car. Val said she'd park up and come in to meet me. I walked off, checked in and waited a few minutes. She didn't come. Before long I had started to wonder what was going on. Wasn't she coming back?

I waited a few more minutes and then heard my phone bleep. It was a text from Val.

'Have a look in your jacket pocket,' it read.

I reached into my pocket and pulled out a pair of red panties! I heard some people giggling and turned around to see two girls looking at me.

'You had a good holiday, didn't you?' one of them piped up.

I laughed my head off. They were right – I'd had a wonderful time in every way.

As I flew home, I thought only of Val and the next time I would see her. I felt as strong as an ox; I could see my life clearly again and I was feeling so much more myself. I thought about her prank too and vowed to get her back when she returned to England. And as sure as eggs is eggs, I did.

'Is my chauffeur going to meet me at the airport?' Val joked down the phone a week later as she was about to board a plane for London. He certainly was... I put my suit on, bought a chauffeur's cap and made a massive placard that read 'SEXY VAL' in huge lettering. Then I set off.

When Val saw me waiting in Arrivals with my placard held high, she nearly fell over with laughter. I'd got her back for her prank, and I felt great knowing we were going to have so much fun together. When we reached my car Val found a large bouquet of red roses on her seat.

Until I met Val, nothing could have persuaded me that I could find the kind of love I'd had with Maggie. To me, it was simply inconceivable. Nobody gets two bites of the cherry, I'd thought. So far as I was concerned, I'd had my time with Maggie and nothing would ever compare to that.

I was wrong and very glad to be wrong. Falling in love with Val made me feel like the luckiest man on the planet. I had to pinch myself quite a few times before I believed that I had been given a second chance at happiness. But it was true, and I felt truly blessed.

Val and I had met in July and after a few months of bliss I came to a decision. I desperately wanted to marry her. We went to stay with some friends in Paris, and I decided I would propose while we were there. I was fully aware that I'd asked Maggie to marry me in Paris, but I didn't think that it mattered because I felt that Maggie would have been happy for me. Anyway, I wasn't planning on asking Val at the top of the Eiffel Tower – that *would* have been weird.

This was about Val and me, not Maggie, and I would do things very differently. I wanted things to be perfect, so I asked my Parisian friends to send me to the best restaurant they knew. We all had dinner in a marvellous place on the river Seine, near St Germain. My friend briefed the owner about my plans, and when the moment came I nodded to the restaurateur, who motioned to all the diners until they went quiet.

The noise died right down and people looked around in confused silence. The owner's daughters came up to our table and announced in French that Monsieur Lane had an announcement to make. Everybody was looking at me. From the wide-eyed, baffled look on Val's face I could tell that she was wondering what on earth was happening.

Then I got down on one knee and produced the ring. Everybody cheered and clapped. People came up to the table and offered their congratulations; it was bliss.

'But I said *no!*' cried Val. My heart skipped a beat. 'Oh go on then,' she said, laughing. 'It is a lovely ring after all!'

She'd got me again, and when I saw the glint in her eye I laughed too. She told me there wasn't a doubt in her mind. That certainty was just another thing we had in common.

CHAPTER 11

BACK TO
BUSINESS

I was in love again... but I still had a job to do up at Beachy Head. With Val in my life, I was more ready than ever to devote myself to the cliff-top patrols.

I'd never deviated from my routine, but had always dreaded the end of the day when I would return home to face the demons I'd temporarily escaped while helping others. Now, I'd moved in with a wonderful woman who was there to greet me when I walked through the door of her house — and before long, her house became 'our house'.

Val knew what I did when she met me; she'd read about me in the papers. From the word go, I was always honest about the fact that I had no intention of stopping my patrols and she had been very clear about her attitude towards them.

I'll never forget her wonderful words. 'If Maggie was alive today,' she said, 'then you and I would never have been together. You'd still be with her and I'd be elsewhere. Maggie's no longer on this planet, but I am, and I'm happy about it. I'm also over the moon that I'm with you. I'm in love with you and obviously that means I don't like the idea of you going up to Beachy Head and putting your life on the line. Now I've found you, I don't want to lose you.'

I wondered what was coming next.

'However, I wouldn't dream of trying to stop you patrolling. I know how much it means to you and I want you to be happy. You wouldn't be the man I fell in love with if you stopped living part of your life because of me. If I told you to stop, you'd never forgive me. You will know when the time has come for you to pack it up, and you will make the decision, not me.'

I couldn't thank her enough for her honesty and understanding. I still thank her today. Now, it was time to go back to work.

★   ★   ★

It was late November. The police were looking for a local girl. She had mental health problems and had gone missing before; now she was missing again. There was a strong chance that she could be suicidal. I was up at the Head and on the look out in case she'd made her way up there. Sure enough, she had.

I came across her soon enough. She was an attractive, very strongly built brunette in her mid-to-late-twenties, and had climbed on to an area of the cliff that was dangerously close to collapsing into the sea. It was a precarious position – not somewhere you'd want to stand for too long, let alone sit. But sitting she was. As usual, the sight of a person on the edge set my adrenaline pumping and my heart racing.

It was a bitterly cold day. I told the police where I was so that they could join me and then I stepped out on to the ledge to join the girl. I was glad she was sitting down, because it meant she couldn't make any sudden movement and jump. At first she hardly responded to me at all. No matter what I said, she repeatedly told me to leave her alone. It wasn't until the police arrived that she started talking – but she didn't want a conversation.

'Fuck off!' she kept screaming. 'Just fuck off and leave me be. Especially you, you bastards.' In her eyes, the 'bastards' were the cops, who were actually a couple of lovely guys. The two officers were prevented by Health and Safety laws from joining the girl and me on the ledge – it was deemed too dangerous – but there was nothing to stop me being there. I wasn't in anyone's employment, so I wasn't flouting any rules.

I was sitting about 3 feet away from her. I knew I needed to get closer, but as I began to inch towards her I became nervous – her size meant that if she decided to go she'd probably be able to take me with her. I was starting to feel nervous now because, deep down, I suspected that I wouldn't be able to stop myself from trying to grab her if she went. What's more, I knew I was literally on shaky ground – this part of the cliff was in danger of collapsing. As I moved closer, the girl became suddenly very aggressive.

'Don't you fucking come any closer!' she screamed, wide eyed and furious. I could tell she meant business, so I stopped dead.

'I'm only trying to help you, sweetheart,' I told her. But it was no use. Anything the police and I said fell on deaf ears. We tried everything – from Maggie's story, to telling her that she wouldn't be in any trouble if she came down, from trying to ask her what the problem was, to assuring her that whatever it was there was help at hand. But our words were met only with aggression.

We weren't going to give up – you can't just walk away from a situation like that. We kept on trying to talk and she kept on telling us to fuck off. Finally however, after about an hour, she began to calm down. Now she was talking rather than screaming. Maybe we were getting somewhere after all...

It was obvious she was very troubled. Up until now, my experience had been that once I'd got someone talking they would open up, say what their problems were and tell me what had brought them to Beachy Head. This girl was different. All she would say was that life was no good and that she'd had enough.

The police knew her name and from what they said next I could tell they had dealt with her before. They changed tack and began talking about a subject that was obviously close to her heart. Food.

'You must be getting hungry now,' they began. 'You're cold. Surely you must want a hot cup of tea and something to eat?'

This seemed to strike a chord. The girl began talking about her favourite food – pizza. Before I knew it, we were all talking pizzas – toppings, bases and who liked what – you name it, we talked about it! The girl seemed to be an utterly different person now that we'd changed the subject. It was as if she'd forgotten that we were up on a cliff edge in the freezing cold and that she was intending to kill herself.

Even she seemed to appreciate the absurdity of the situation. After a good ten minutes of pizza talk, she suddenly burst into laughter.

'What on earth is going on?' she howled. 'Why the hell are we all talking about pizzas?'

'You tell us,' we said, laughing with her. 'Now why don't you think about coming down so we can go and get one?'

It had been two-and-a-half hours and only now were we making progress. Still, it had been worth it. If talking pizza was what it was going to take to stop someone killing themselves, then I was prepared to discuss toppings till kingdom come.

She had let me get a little closer. We were just at the point where she was calm enough to agree to come down – and that's when it all started to go wrong. The radio belonging to one of the policemen went off. Whoever was in charge back at the station was getting annoyed at the amount of time it was taking the officers to deal with the incident. As far he was concerned, they should have been off doing something else by now. The officer tried to assure the boss that the job was nearly done, but his superior officer wasn't hearing any of it.

Within ten minutes, the boss and two more policemen were marching up the hill towards us. Shit, I thought, Here we go! We'd all done so well so far, but I had the feeling that all of our good work was about to come undone. I was right.

The boss arrived at the edge and started screaming at the girl.

'I've had enough of this,' he yelled angrily. 'If you're going to jump, go ahead and do it. If you're not, then come off!'

Psychology obviously wasn't his specialist subject! I couldn't believe this man was carrying on in such a way. For everyone's sake, I wished he'd shut up. As soon as he spoke, the girl moved even closer to the edge.

If I wasn't so anxious to keep an eye on the girl, I would have put my head in my hands. He had had more to say, too, but this time it was to me.

'Who the hell do you think you are?' he shouted.

I explained who I was and that I did regular patrols in order to save lives.

'Get down from there now,' he shot back sharply. 'I don't want the public there.'

'I'm not going anywhere, and you can't make me. I'm trying to help this young lady,' I shouted back. 'I'm no psychologist – I'm just Joe Public – but I can tell you that the way you're talking to her is not helping things. I suggest you take your two extra officers and get the hell out of here because you're no good to us!'

Needless to say, this didn't go down too well. He told me I had a nerve to talk to him in such a way and asked me who the hell I thought I was. I told him I thought I was nobody but an ordinary guy trying to help. I added that I knew he was doing his job, but that I thought he was doing it very badly. I told him that the two police officers and I could get the girl down if only he and the other officers left us alone.

'You've got half an hour,' he said grudgingly, and marched back down the hill. I'd ruffled his feathers, for sure, but it got the result I wanted. Now we could finally focus on the girl again.

'Well, we still haven't got any pizza, have we?' I said once the boss had gone. It took a little while, but before long the girl was laughing again. We were back on track to saving her, I hoped. 'You don't really want to die, do you?' I said. 'The only thing you want to kill is a pizza – I bet you could murder one!'

She laughed her head off at that. But whenever I suggested she came down, her faced turned serious once more. She was nervous of the police.

'Can we come to a compromise?' I asked her. 'I can see that you don't want to go with these officers, but if I can persuade them to walk away, will you walk down to the car park? You can go to your car, get your things, and go peacefully with the police. They won't manhandle you, I promise.'

'All right,' she said. 'I'll come if we can do it that way.'

I breathed a sigh of relief and turned to the two officers.

'Well?' I said, 'Is that a deal? No handcuffs, no heavy stuff. She'll walk back to the car and go peacefully…'

One of the officers radioed back to the boss. The deal was on. The policemen walked away.

We stepped off the ledge. It was good to know that the ground wasn't going to collapse into the sea and even better to know that the girl was safe. However, now the police came back to tell me they would walk her from here.

'Oh no you won't,' I said firmly. 'We had a deal, remember?'

The police insisted on walking behind the girl to make sure she was safe, but they agreed to keep 30 yd back. The girl seemed happy enough with this. Before we parted I told her that I would walk down to the other car park to get my car and then drive over to meet her and say goodbye. She nodded.

As I was driving my car towards the girl's, I looked across the headland from the road. I could hardly believe my eyes. There was a police car halfway up the hill. It was behind some bushes and out of sight of the girl who was walking towards them. Immediately, I sensed that they had set a trap for her. So much for our deal.

I got out of the car and began running towards them. But it was too late. By the time I got there two police officers had jumped from behind a bush and grabbed the girl. Naturally, she was beside herself with panic and rage. As soon as she realised she had been deceived, she began shouting and screaming – and that gave them the excuse they needed to arrest her.

They swept her legs from under her and she went crashing to the ground. In a split second one of the officers was on top of her and putting the handcuffs on.

'You bastards,' she was screaming. 'You fucking *bastards!* You promised, you promised…'

'Leave her,' I shouted, 'leave her alone. There's no need for that.'

'Oh yes there is,' said the boss. He told me it was his responsibility to manage the situation and that the girl could easily have run back and jumped. From the way she'd been when we'd made the deal, it was pretty obvious her frame of mind had changed. If anything was going to make her want to run and jump again, it was being manhandled by the police.

The girl turned to look at me. She was hysterical, exactly as she had been when I met her hours before. 'You're a fucking bastard,' she yelled at me viciously. 'You knew this was going to happen and you betrayed me!'

There was no point in proclaiming my innocence to her. I could see how she thought I was in on what had happened, but I was absolutely mortified about how things had turned out, and gutted that she thought I'd tricked her.

Once again, I appealed to the officer in charge to stop what was happening.

'I have to do this,' he shot back, flatly. I was livid. The girl screamed and writhed.

'No you don't,' I shouted. 'There's a humane way of doing these things, and this isn't it. You're treating her like an animal!'

'It's for her own safety!' he retorted. She may well have become very agitated, but only because she'd been betrayed. In my opinion, there's no way that girl wasn't going to keep her side of the bargain.

The police bundled her into the car and drove off quickly as she hollered and cried. I never saw her again. I assume they took her to the station – and I don't know what treatment she received there. All I know is that I witnessed a troubled girl who was obviously struggling with her mental health, and she was treated like a common criminal. The last thing a person in a fragile mental state needs is to be manhandled, cuffed and bundled into a car.

I felt sick to my heart at what I had witnessed and as I drove home I was so upset that there was a moment where I wondered if all my patrolling was worth it. For the first time I thought about giving up.

I walked into the house drained and very upset. But after a stiff drink, a big cuddle and a chat with Val I'd managed to put some perspective on what had happened. When I thought about it, I felt it was only the boss who had so unnecessarily turned things sour. The two lovely Bobbies had been wonderful and I don't doubt that together we would have managed to get the girl down without a scene. I wasn't bitter about the police, I was annoyed at what I considered to be the insensitivity of the boss, and I had to keep that in mind. I had to refrain from making any sweeping comments about the incident to friends, because the last thing I wanted was it getting back to the press that I thought the police were horrible, or doing a bad job. Most of them do a fantastic job. It just seems that it's those at the top – confident that they know best – who are the problem in so many areas of life. This incident was just a classic example of authority getting in the way of humanity and common sense.

In the future I would encounter problems of a similar nature, though not with the police. But whenever bad situations arose, I would always tell myself that for one arsehole in charge there are 20 wonderful people doing their best!

*   *   *

It was around this time that *Songs of Praise* got in touch. They wanted to film me talking about my experiences in Eastbourne and then move up to Beachy Head. Thinking the nationwide coverage could help my campaign, I agreed to it. Jonathan Edwards interviewed me and at first everything went very smoothly. As we approached Beachy Head with the intention of filming some reconstructions of incidents I'd been involved in, I explained that if a real incident were to happen while we were up there, they would have to turn their cameras off out of respect.

No sooner had we unpacked all of the camera equipment than I spotted a man standing at the edge. I told them I would have to go on alone. Obligingly, the crew stopped filming.

The man was middle-aged and in a complete state. Marital issues were at the heart of the matter: his wife had left him and he didn't know what to do. He only knew that he wanted to end it all.

His body language was bad. Hands shaking, fists clenched, he paced around in a very agitated manner, talking to himself about dying, crying, blaming his wife for everything. His tone was even and calm, but his words were worrying nevertheless. By now, I had been joined by the coastguard, who kept talking about Health & Safety issues; he was worried that I might end up doing something dangerous, or put myself at risk, while trying to help this man. I didn't think the risks I took were any business of his and I tried to tell him to leave me alone, but he wasn't having any of it. After all, it was his job to make sure things were safe. However, I was more concerned about saving a life, so I just ignored him and got on with it.

'Is this an official incident?' I asked him. It wasn't. That was a good thing. By 'official incident', I meant one where the police had been called out because someone was missing. It is an official incident if someone is in mental care and they go missing, or if anyone calls the police to say that a loved one may be up at Beachy Head. It doesn't matter who is involved in an incident – the chaplains, the coastguard, me or anyone else – once the police take over there is nothing anyone else can do. When the police arrive at the scene, it is their job to take the person to a police cell for safe keeping under the Mental Health Act. There they remain until a doctor is free to assess them and decide whether they should be sectioned or released.

I'd been through my usual routine with the man. I'd told him all about Maggie. At last, he was starting to calm down, so I asked him if he was confined by the mental health system. He wasn't. Nevertheless, I suspected that the coastguard would soon be calling the police, if he hadn't done so already. I knew they would be here soon.

'Listen,' I said forcefully. 'Can we get down to brass tacks here? Within the next 15 minutes the cops will be arriving, and you're going to be taken away to a police cell. You won't be arrested but it won't be pleasant. You will be locked up until they have time to deal with you.'

I had his full attention now.

'Unless you feel you really need help,' I continued, 'I would go back to your friends and do your best to talk to

143

your wife. If you need the police, and if you need a doctor, then stay here. Otherwise, get in your car. Now.'

I didn't really have the right to be doing this – it was a police matter, after all. Yet I had a strong feeling that this guy would be better off where he'd come from, so took the decision to urge him to leave. I walked him back to the car park where the *Songs of Praise* camera crew were waiting. A friend of mine was with them – he was there to act in the reconstructions – and before we said goodbye to the man we asked him where he was going.

'Brighton,' he replied before thanking me and driving away.

The coastguard soon caught up with us and asked where the man had gone.

'He's gone back to Eastbourne,' replied my friend.

We threw them off the scent and I'm pleased to say I never saw or heard of the guy again. Not that I would always let someone go so easily. I did it then because I felt that, having talked to hundreds of troubled people, I was by now experienced enough to judge how much of a danger to him or herself someone was. In fact, I'd come up with a system for categorising incidents.

A 'Category One' was what I called a 'real jumper'. These were individuals who were quite obviously about to go. They were deadly serious and once I spotted them I could immediately tell it was truly a matter of life and death – with those incidents I would always have the feeling that they could go in a split second.

A 'Category Two' was someone who obviously had serious problems, who may well jump if left to their own devices, but didn't seem so completely determined to do it. With them, I always had the feeling that they were still able to listen to reason.

'Category Threes' were people I felt just needed a bit of TLC. They were troubled, for sure – anyone pacing the edge of a cliff and thinking about death is certainly that – but from their body language it was plain they simply needed a good talk and somebody to reassure them that they were not alone in the world.

Despite his body language, once I had started talking to the man from Brighton, I quickly realised he was a 'Category Three'. If he was in any other category, I would have simply kept him safe until the police arrived.

The man was gone. The coastguard was gone. The police were probably looking around Eastbourne. The only ones remaining were me, a BBC crew and Jonathan Edwards. All of them were gobsmacked – we'd come up to reconstruct an incident or two for the cameras and they'd ended up witnessing a real save. Some of them were still stunned as we got on with the reconstructions.

In the middle of filming, we were stopped. The coastguard had obviously been doing his job very well because he'd told the council we were filming. Before we knew it, the council were on to us to demand that we stopped filming the reconstructions. They also insisted we didn't use any of the footage that had been taken. It was very annoying because we'd been filming with the best of intentions – we wanted to raise awareness about the problems up at Beachy Head.

It was time to go home.

Songs of Praise aired (minus the reconstructions) and I was delighted by the emails and letters of support I received as a result of it. As always, the kindness of strangers inspired me to keep up the work – whatever obstacles I met with.

CHAPTER 12

TROUBLE WITH
THE CHAPLAINS

In 2004, around the same time as me, the Beachy Head Chaplaincy Team began their mission. Their Frontline Team patrol the cliffs for around 100 hours a week, and their aims are the same as mine. The difference between the chaplains and myself was that I wasn't part of an organisation – the chaplains are a church-based group with volunteers coming from various churches in the area – and I didn't wear a uniform or drive a marked van. Additionally, I wasn't funded. Not major differences, for sure, and we certainly had one thing in common – the desire to stop people dying up at Beachy Head.

The team is funded primarily by contributions from the public and before the Maggie Lane Trust had officially got going I gave the chaplains a considerable sum of money to help them keep going. At the time they were short of funds, and were very grateful for the £500 that I donated from Maggie's fund.

In the early days of my patrols, my relationship with the chaplains was very amicable – none of us had a problem with each other. It's always been my thinking that it doesn't matter who's saving lives – the chaplains, the police, the coastguard, me, a local dog walker or Father Christmas – so long as they are being saved. I assumed that all of the chaplains felt the same way. Over time, I would learn that I was wrong.

Most of the chaplains I met on patrol up at the edge were wonderful, kind-hearted people. However, over time it became apparent to me that certain chaplains did not like my presence at Beachy Head one bit. Much to my regret, it was around the beginning of 2006 that my previously good relationship with them began to deteriorate.

Things fell apart slowly – as relationships often do. Certain chaplains became increasingly agitated about the press coverage I was getting for my work. I pointed out that a media blackout at San Francisco's Golden Gate Bridge – as much a suicide hotspot as Beachy Head – hadn't affected suicide figures one jot. I also drew attention to the fact that yearly figures have fluctuated since records began and that they actually went down during some of the time that I was patrolling. Furthermore, I don't recall anyone up at Beachy Head being talked down and announcing that it was Keith Lane who had drawn them there in the first place. Still, my arguments made no difference to the way some chaplains felt about me. It seemed as if they considered me more of a hindrance than a help, although I couldn't work out why. I was saving people, after all. Wasn't that the point?

One day I was talking to a chaplain up at the Head. He told me that he felt it was his – and the other chaplains' – God-given right to be up there. According to him, it was them, and only them, who should be up there saving people. Since I'd been helping to fund them, I found this hard to take. But I let it pass, feeling that the matter was too trivial to bother getting into an argument about. I wondered if there was an element of jealousy involved – the media were approaching me left, right and centre. I only agreed to interviews to help my campaign for 24-hour cover and to raise money for the Maggie Lane Trust. As time passed, I began to get the feeling that not everybody thought that my patrols were helpful.

A big search was on. A girl who'd been placed in mental care had gone missing. I was on my usual patrol and, bumping into one of the chaplains, I asked him if I could help in any way. We were up at Shooters Hill, an area near Beachy Head, and he said he'd be grateful for my assistance. As we spoke, he received a radio call. Afterwards, he suggested we went in opposite directions along the cliff. Accordingly, I started walking up the hill. However, when I looked around to check on his progress, I saw the chaplain running back to his car and driving off.

I went back to my car and drove after the chaplain. As I came close to Beachy Head, I could see the police and the chaplain's van. They'd found the woman and had begun the process of trying to talk her down. I parked up and walked towards them.

There were three or four police officers, some coastguards, and a few chaplains – around 15 people in all – maintaining a safe distance from the girl. They have to remain at a certain distance for Health and Safety reasons. If the coastguards want to get closer, they have to be harnessed up.

As I came closer a policeman stopped me. 'Where do you think you're going?' he said suspiciously.

'I've been helping the chaplains with the search,' I answered. 'Please let me approach…'

'Stay where you are,' he interrupted. 'We are the professionals, *not* you.'

I didn't object. I offered to help if they needed me. But at the same time I felt it sad that I was not allowed to approach the woman. Professionals they may all have been, but they were restricted by rules and regulations that didn't apply to me. I was always free to approach whoever I wanted, to get as close as I wanted, and being close to people seemed to work for me. In addition to this, as far as I was aware, none of the people present had lost people to suicide. Sure, I didn't have professional qualifications, but I did have experience, and it made it easy for me to empathise with troubled people up at the Head – people tended to trust me because I wasn't a figure of authority, I was just a guy who'd lost his wife. I don't think I'm better than anyone, but it hurt a little to be dismissed so casually. I really wanted to help.

'If you really want to be useful,' the policeman said, 'you can help my officers form a cordon to stop passers-by from trying to look.'

Fair enough. I joined the cordon.

The rescue was taking a long time. The coastguards, the police and the chaplains were all getting harnessed up so that they could inch towards the girl. I could see exactly what was happening and, from my point of view, this was not a good rescue. I felt that the presence of so many people would be intimidating for the woman at the edge.

It was a bitterly cold day. One of the policemen walked to the Beachy Head pub and came back with a tray full of teas and coffees to keep people buoyed up and warm. He passed one to everyone involved in the rescue, and then handed the rest out to everyone involved in forming the cordon. But he didn't hand one to me.

Oh well, I thought, Perhaps he's miscounted. While everyone stood around warming themselves up with their drinks, I kept receiving the odd glance. Then a few people started sniggering and laughing. It didn't take a genius to work out what they found so funny. They were amused that I was the only one without a drink. Their behaviour was petty and pathetic, but there's no point in denying that it really hurt.

A few people were making it very clear that they didn't want me around. I knew that I wasn't welcome, so I simply walked away from the cliff and drove off.

I reflected on that incident for quite a while. I felt humiliated and let down. The coastguard who had ended up grabbing the girl won an award because he nearly fell, even though he was harnessed up. I firmly believe that with fewer people around and a little more patience and talking, the girl could have been talked down without any trauma. It's when Health and Safety raises its ugly head that common sense goes out of the window.

I was no longer wanted and it didn't feel good but nothing was going to stop me patrolling – not even missing out on a cuppa!

In spite of that unpleasantness, I was in love and happy again. Under the supervision of the doctor, and with Val's tremendous support, I managed to come off Prozac and start living as the old Keith once more. I didn't want the pills any longer. I wanted reality – and I couldn't wait for Val to become my wife.

CHAPTER 13
WEDDING BELLS

'You're old enough to know what you're doing,' my daughter told me.

'And you're old enough to know what you're doing too,' Val's kids told her.

'But are you *sure*?' they all asked.

We were sure all right. We picked a day in March 2005, and began planning. We hired a wonderful function room at the The Pier Hotel in Eastbourne, and off we went. It was fabulous. Everything fell into place beautifully. We had a band, all of our friends and family were there and there was a feeling of magic in the air.

We planned it so that as she walked down the aisle, Val would sing the first verse of 'When You Tell Me That You Love Me' by Diana Ross and I would sing the second. Then, once she arrived at my side, we would sing the third verse together. When we held hands and sang to each other and there wasn't a dry eye in the place.

Afterwards, we danced until 2 am before heading off to our honeymoon suite. We hadn't asked for presents, as we had planned a trip around the world. Instead, our mates had clubbed together and handed over great wads of cash for us to use on our honeymoon. Two newlyweds counting out hundreds of fives, tens and twenties on the bed must have been quite a sight. We were throwing it around and laughing together as usual. We were about to take off on a dream trip and we couldn't have done it without our wonderful friends.

Val and I jetted off for six weeks, taking in Los Angeles, New Zealand and Australia before flying to Hong Kong and home. To use a cliché, it was the trip of a lifetime. We drove through the Australian outback, we swam with dolphins in the wild, we sped around on hover jets and, more than anything, we fell even more deeply in love.

Everything had happened so fast that at times it felt quite surreal. I'd be in the middle of something and have to pause for a few seconds to take stock of things and reflect on how lucky I was. Part of me worried that it would all be snatched away from me at any moment, that this bliss was all a dream. But the longer it went on, the more I had to accept that it was all wonderfully true – that Val's love was wonderfully real. That's life I suppose – one minute you're down in the shit, the next you're up in the clouds.

I believe in fate. It may sound odd, but I believe that part of the reason Maggie left this world was to help me. By this, I mean that her passing freed me up to get on with my work of saving people at Beachy Head. And after all the pain of losing her began to subside a little, I was able to get on with my life without having to deal with the trauma she had been putting me through. I believe that, despite everything Maggie and I went through together, she felt dreadfully guilty about her behaviour. I think it tore her up that she was causing me such distress, just as I'm sure she felt bad about the damage she was doing to herself. The problem was, she didn't feel able to change it, alone or with my help, and needed to escape the pain. It still makes me feel sad to say it, but I believe that in some way Maggie was destined to go, and I was destined to fall in love with someone who would be able to look after me as much as I look after them.

Maggie's death changed me as a man. It changed my personality completely. I have been forced to consider life and death in such a horribly raw way, and in the long run I have gained a fresh perspective on life as a whole. I'm wiser than I was before and the little things annoy me less. I have a lot to thank Maggie for, even to this day. In some ways, I even thank her for her death – I wouldn't have gone on to save the lives of so many people if it hadn't happened. Ultimately, though it may sound a strange thing to say, Maggie saved a lot of lives by dying.

I would never have wished Maggie's life to be over. While

she was alive, she was my world and there is still a huge place in my heart for her. But my life is with Val now. I can only be grateful for the way things have turned out and thankful that Maggie gave me the opportunity to help others as I have. It's the only way of looking at such a tragedy. If I didn't think of it as something that was almost 'meant to be', then I would never be able to move on.

One of my reasons for writing this book is that I want to give hope to people who have lost loved ones to suicide. When Maggie died I thought my life was over too. I thought it was the end and I carried on thinking like that for a long time. But gradually I began to think differently – and then Val came along and saved me. I'm not here to say that I turned my life around and that others can do the same. It's not that simple. I didn't turn my life around – circumstances did. Call it fate, call it chance, but without it I might not have got through. Sure, I tried to help myself and succeeded to a certain extent. But it was chance that pulled me up and gave me my life back. I truly believe that if you hang on in there, circumstances will conspire to help you. Some people don't have to wait as long as I did; others have to be patient for longer. The point is, a positive can always be made out of a negative; suicide is one massive negative to turn around, but it can be done.

If it happened to me – just an ordinary bloke – there's no reason why it shouldn't happen to anyone else who is grief-stricken.

⋆   ⋆   ⋆

In 2006, it was official. After nearly two years of planning, the Maggie Lane Trust was up and running as a charity. We'd already raised a lot of money from my media work; members of the public had given us money left, right and centre. We began sending out newsletters and giving money to the chaplains. We were also delighted to have the funds to buy searchlights for them. In time, however, it became clear that although we shared the same goal, we had different ways of approaching it.

⋆   ⋆   ⋆

I could see she was a determined lady. A 'Category One'. She was in her early forties, standing in a long, dark raincoat with the toes of her flat, black shoes jutting right over the edge of the cliff. It was a terrifying sight.

I approached her very, very cautiously. As I got nearer, I could see tears streaming down her face. She didn't move a muscle, but simply stared fixedly out to sea with a frightening look of resolve about her.

No matter what I said, I received no response. She wouldn't look at me, she wouldn't nod or give any acknowledgment of my presence. I knew she might go at any moment and there was nothing I could do if she decided to. Moreover, she was way too close to the edge for me to try and grab her – any quick movement could have made her lose balance and fall, or simply panic and jump.

With Val in my life, I still desperately wanted to talk people down, but I'd become a little more cautious about going so close to the edge.

The police must have been called. They turned up but hung back after they recognised me. This was not a situation where rushing in was going to achieve anything – and could easily end in tragedy.

I carried on talking. I tried every rhetorical trick I knew. Up until now I'd always managed to get people to engage in some sort of conversation, even if they were only telling me to fuck off! This woman's lips were sealed for a very long time.

I couldn't grab her, so I had to keep talking. Eventually, she spoke five words. 'I just want to die,' she said, with a quiet force that chilled me to the bone. It was obvious she meant it. I carried on trying to persuade her that this might not be the only way for her. But each time she responded, she repeated the same line.

I began to consider my options. Talking was achieving nothing, and as each moment passed I became more convinced that she was going to go over the edge. I had no choice but to try and get hold of her somehow.

Very slowly, I began to edge closer to her. She didn't seem to notice at first, so I kept on moving – as slowly as possible. I hoped that her focus on the horizon would make her oblivious to my movements. It was too much to hope for. When I was about 4 feet from her, she noticed me in the corner of her eye and in that moment she lifted her leg and began to step forward into thin air.

I lunged towards her, hitting her from the right. I clasped my hand over her face and knocked her sideways and backwards. As we fell to the ground, I felt my right leg slide over the edge.

My heart leaped as I scrambled desperately to pull my body to safety while the police grabbed the woman. I got up, brushed myself down and breathed in and out. It had been a close one – almost too close for comfort.

The woman didn't struggle, so there was no need to handcuff her. Once the police helped her to her feet, she simply stood there silently.

'Thanks a lot. You did a good job,' said one of the officers.

I imagined that the woman would be angry with me and expected her to start shouting in the way that others had before. Nothing. Her face was expressionless.

'Well, we're going back to the station now,' said one of the officers. As they turned to go, one of the officers looked at me and said something that still touches me now. 'We do appreciate what you do up here, Keith.'

He didn't need to say any more. To hear those words from a police officer meant the world to me, especially after some of the unsavoury encounters I'd experienced of late. In fact, I was slightly shocked.

I remained near the edge as they walked away, and only once they'd left did it begin to hit me how close I'd come to death. Before this incident, people had often asked me whether I would take a lunge in order to try and save somebody – if it were a matter of life and death. My reply was always, 'I don't know until it happens.'

I didn't know until that woman went to take a step, but then I had my answer. It seemed that, yes, I was prepared to put myself in the way of someone.

It had happened in a split second. My adrenaline was already pumping like crazy because I was so convinced she was going to jump, so when it came to it I think the level of adrenaline and stress made me act on autopilot. I wasn't thinking of anything other than the woman and I certainly didn't *decide* to take such a risk – it felt as if my body did the work for me in a fraction of a second. Before I knew it, I was scrambling to safety after having come so close to falling.

Now the adrenaline had worn off and I was thinking logically about what had just happened, I began to shake quite severely. Knowing that I could have died was a very strange sensation indeed – not a feeling I'd want to have too often!

There was only one thing for it. I took myself over to the Beachy Head pub and bought a large whisky. I sat there for as long as it took me to calm down, finished my drink and left. I looked up the hill towards the cliff edge, scanned it with my binoculars and began walking back up.

★　　★　　★　　★　　★

We all have rights. The question of whether or not a person has the right to kill him- or herself is a difficult one to answer. I believe that, ultimately, it's everyone's right to do what they want to do. If someone wants to die, who am I to say, 'You can't kill yourself'?

People often ask me if I think that Maggie was acting selfishly when she died. I always say 'no', because I think she had mental health problems that made her act irrationally – if you're in a state of mind where you can't perceive the consequences of what you're doing, if you can't see that you're going to hurt others, then surely you can't be accused of being selfish? To many people who are in a logical, healthy frame of mind, it can seem like a selfish act. After all, suicide hurts so many of the people left behind.

But there are lots of things in life that hurt other people and we have the right to do them. People leave their wives and husbands, have affairs, say terrible things. I say that people do have the right to commit suicide, but I also believe strongly that anyone in such a frame of mind is not thinking logically and has gone beyond the point where they can really grasp the dire consequences of such an act.

So if I think that people have the right to die, then why did I spend so much time trying to stop them? The answer is simple. Just as people have the right to attempt suicide, I have the right to try and stop them. I believe that everybody deserves a second chance in life. Often I talked people down, but in some cases, such as the woman whom I've just mentioned, I physically stopped them from jumping. She may have gone away, reflected on things and decided she was glad to be alive. She may have decided she still wanted to die and ended her life later on. Maybe my presence was her lucky day; maybe not.

Either way, I've dealt with suicide on so many levels – my wife killed herself, I thought about killing myself (and thanked my lucky stars that I didn't) – and I have experienced the grief of losing someone. Armed with that knowledge, I always felt that I was doing a potentially good thing by making the decision to stop someone dying. I was giving them a chance to reconsider. After all, if someone dies, they don't get to regret it. If they have a chance to think again, they may regret having considered it in the first place. If they end up happy to be alive, then that's justification enough for me having brought them away from that edge.

CHAPTER 14

A CRUSHING BLOW

It was a beautiful day in May 2006. I had just arrived at Maggie's cross, a place known as a 'good jumping spot'. People milled around, enjoying the weather. Among them was a lovely looking girl sitting on the grass. She was about 10 ft from the edge, had dark hair, glasses and a pretty round face, and as I walked past her she gave me a smile and took a sip from her water bottle. Nothing to worry about here, I thought.

I'd already spotted a woman sitting near the edge farther down the hill, towards the lighthouse, so I set off in that direction. But before I got close, she stood up and strolled on. She was OK too.

Instead of continuing my walk past the lighthouse as I normally would, I had an impulse to turn around and walk back to where I'd come from. I don't know why – perhaps it was Maggie trying to tell me something – but I felt compelled to go back and retrace my steps. I walked back to where I'd just come from.

As I approaching Maggie's spot again, I noticed that the pretty girl with the water bottle had moved. Now, she was sitting right near the edge, still sipping from her water bottle, but rocking backwards and forwards as if she was building herself up to something. Shit, I thought, she's in trouble.

Her rocking made me so nervous that I called out to her before I got close.

'Hello, my darling,' I shouted brightly. 'Are you OK?'

She turned and looked at me as I came up to her.

'No,' she said. 'I've had enough.'

I asked her if she wanted to talk. Perhaps she could explain a bit more?

'I've been a manic depressive all my life and I can't take any more. I really need to end the pain,' she said frankly, yet with a deeply melancholic voice.

Manic depression, also known as bipolar disorder, is different from depression. Some people are depressed for most of their life, while others go through periods of depression in response to life stresses. Manic depression is viewed as a chemical imbalance in the brain that normally requires lifelong treatment in the form of therapy, medication, or both. People who suffer from bipolar disorder experience a range of symptoms that are hard to control, from low periods of crushing depression, to high – or 'manic'

– periods of intense energy and productivity that can lead to bizarre and inappropriate behaviour. If left untreated, manic depression often leads to suicide.

When this girl told me she was manic-depressive, I knew she must have endured many ups and downs over the years. I wanted to know her story, but she looked so close to jumping that I decided to cut to the chase.

'Listen,' I said, 'just listen to my story for two minutes…'

After I'd told her about Maggie's, I pointed at her cross. 'I put that there for my wife,' I said. 'Can you really go ahead and jump? If you did, it would destroy me.'

She looked at me and backed away from the edge a little. We sat down together on one of the step-like ledges that lead down to the cliff edge and began to talk.

Her name was Bella. She was from the Croydon area and was a Buddhist. She'd spent much of her life in and out of psychiatric hospitals and had been on so many different drugs for her condition that she could barely remember them all. Bella had really tried to help herself and the authorities had tried too, but it seemed that nothing worked. She kept on swinging between the highs and the lows and she'd had enough of trying to cope.

Despite her depressed state, Bella was still hugely interested in me, and showed incredible empathy when discussing Maggie. She was clearly so sorry to hear what I'd been through. At times it felt like *she* was doing the counselling! Bella was such a wonderful person that it made me even more determined to help her. Yet she was equally determined to end it all. She told me how close she was to her sister and I asked her if she could really put her sister through losing her.

'She'll understand,' was her simple reply.

'I don't think she will,' I stressed. '*Nobody* understands how a loved one can do such a thing. You're feeling pretty messed up inside right now – it's quite possible that even you don't fully comprehend why you want to die. Even if you do, nobody else can climb inside your head and fully understand those thoughts. Why don't you come away from here with me so that we can talk to your sister together?'

Bella paused for thought. After a while she agreed to come to my car and let me run her to the station so she could go back to her flat. When we got to the car park, she turned and looked back up at the cliff thoughtfully.

'What are you thinking?' I asked.

'Keith,' she began, 'you're a lovely man and I know you mean well, but I just want to die. I can't stand this pain any more.'

Although it wasn't for me to make assumptions about her illness, I believe it is always worth trying to find a solution to a problem, no matter how big it is. I told her so. 'Let's talk some more,' I suggested, 'and see if we can't come up with a few ideas that may help.'

An ice cream van pulled up in the car park. It turned out that Bella loved ice cream, so I bought us the biggest 99 flakes I could get. We sat in my car, licking our ice creams and talking. By the end of the conversation, I felt that we'd made great progress. She's safe at last, I thought.

Bella told me that the Croydon Health Authority would soon notice she was missing, so to avoid the possibility of the police becoming involved, she allowed me to call her doctor, let him know where she was and tell him that she was safe.

Bella's doctor was concerned, but I assured him that she was about to get back on the train. We agreed that he would meet her at the station and he promised he would phone me to tell me she'd arrived safely.

While we waited at the train station, I tried to persuade Bella to call her sister and let her know what was happening. She wouldn't, but she promised me she would really go home. Just to be sure I walked over and asked the guard on the train to call the police immediately if Bella got off at any stop before Croydon.

I'll never forget saying goodbye to Bella. She gave me a huge hug and a smile to die for. 'You're the kindest man I've ever met, you know,' she said affectionately.

'Don't you worry about me, sweetheart,' I smiled. 'Just go back, get them to reassess your drugs, and get better. You'll work things out.'

Bella stepped on to the train and waved to me from her seat. As the train pulled away, she blew me a kiss.

I felt great. I knew I'd done everything I could. I'd saved a wonderful girl, made sure she was safe, and now she was going back home where she belonged. Elated, I drove back to Beachy Head. Once again, it had all been worth it.

The doctor called to let me know Bella had arrived. They'd had a chat and she was booked in for a drug reassessment the next day. I had developed a real affection for this girl, and asked the doctor if he minded letting me know if she turned up for the appointment. He promised me he would. The call came the next day, a Friday. The assessment had gone smoothly. Bella was back in her flat. All was well.

On Saturday, I went to play golf after my morning patrol. As I drove back to the Head for my 'afternoon shift' I noticed coastguards up at the cliff edge. Oh no, I thought, someone's gone over. Although the coastguards might be up there for a number of reasons, I knew they were always called when a body needed to be retrieved.

I tried to walk up and see what was going on, but the police had formed a cordon around the area. After my previous experience, there was no way I was going to try and get involved. Instead, I walked to a point where I could look over the cliff using my binoculars.

There was a body down there, but it was too far away for me to make out any features. All I could see was the coastguards putting it into a black bag so that they could remove it. At this point, I became highly anxious. I had regularly thought about Bella since Thursday – meeting her had really moved me – and although I was sure she was OK, I wanted to be sure it wasn't her.

I asked a chaplain who was standing nearby if it was a woman, and if it was Bella. It was a woman, but it wasn't her – there was a different name on the bag that the victim had left at the top of the cliff.

Even though it was terrible that someone had died, it was a huge relief to know that it wasn't Bella. It sounds strange, but knowing someone for even a short space of time can make you care about them more than you would a stranger. It's just human nature, I suppose.

Two days later was 16 May – my birthday – and I was having a few drinks at home with Val and her daughter. I'll never forget what happened next. Val popped out of the room for something, and my mobile phone rang while she was gone.

'Your number was on my sister's phone,' said a woman's voice.

'Well, who's your sister?' I replied.

'Bella.'

'Oh, Bella!' I said as I realised what was happening. 'I spoke to her at Beachy Head on Thursday. How's she doing?'

There was a pause.

'Well, I'm afraid Bella died at Beachy Head on Saturday.'

I froze. Later, Val's daughter would tell me I went white with shock. She knew something was wrong straight away and called Val back into the room.

I was so shaken that I couldn't speak. I was trying to follow what the voice on the end of the line was saying, but I simply couldn't take it on board. Bella's sister was attempting to tell me what had happened, but even though she was speaking clearly, to me it sounded like mumbo jumbo. I was dumbstruck. I apologised for not being able to talk and we arranged to meet a couple of days later.

Val and I met Bella's sister up at Beachy Head. We took flowers with us and threw them over the edge at the point Bella had jumped from. There were lots of tears, but Bella's sister showed incredible strength. With her permission we took photos of the spot, and of the flowers being thrown, so that we could feature Bella on the Maggie Lane Trust website — our idea was that Bella's story might move people to think twice about suicide.

I felt terrible about what had happened, and couldn't help feeling I had failed Bella and her sister in some way. 'I'm so sorry I couldn't save your sister,' I said to her. Her response showed immense kindness and humanity.

'You couldn't have been kinder,' she said sweetly. 'You did all you could. Perhaps Bella's time was up...'

Still, I found it hard not to dwell on what I might have missed. I kept thinking — was there something more I could have said to prevent Bella from ending her life? It wasn't until I attended the inquest into her death that I found out just how complex Bella's life had been. She had many problems, some of which paralleled Maggie's. She had suffered from mental illness throughout her life and she was filled with many demons that kept on coming back to haunt her. Both

Maggie and Bella had reached to the stage where they were simply exhausted from coping rather than living. Like Maggie, I think Bella had reached the point where all she wanted was to be at peace. Like Maggie too, I think Bella's tragic case was one where she was almost destined to go – no matter what anyone tried to do, she was determined to die.

Hearing the story of Bella's life made me immensely sad and really brought home to me how Maggie must have felt. It was painful to be thinking about Maggie and Bella at the same time, yet it gave me more of an insight into long-term depression and the motives for suicide. Ultimately, this would not only help me find peace with myself about Maggie, but would also help me into talk with more understanding to other people who were suffering. Bella's case was a tragedy I will never be able to forget.

*   *   *

Later that year, around September, I would encounter a woman at the edge who was suffering from great loss. She was in her mid-40s and her husband had recently died from a heart attack. They had been together since they were teenagers. Her face was so utterly sad that she hardly needed to speak for me to understand what she was going through.

'I just can't face life without him,' she said, her voice soft and gentle. 'We did everything together and now he's gone I don't know what to do.'

She felt that rather than remain alone in this world she

wanted to try and join him in the next. I knew exactly what she meant. I'd had precisely that thought a thousand times since Maggie died. I told her my story and stressed that I'd known the same sadness and pain. 'Do you feel that your heart is bursting out of your body?' I asked her.

She nodded. 'There's just so much pain – I can't live with such loneliness.'

I talked about the isolation I had felt. I talked about having walked down the street feeling like the loneliest person in the world. Every time I spoke she nodded as if to say, 'That's exactly what I've been through.'

By talking about my experience, I was reminding her of all of her negative feelings in order to help her discover that she was not alone in her pain. After some time, I proposed to her that instead of killing herself she might find a way through her grief by talking to others. I suggested that she shared her bereavement with me.

She described what she'd been through since losing her husband. The loneliness, the strange things that people say, the anger – she told me exactly what she was thinking with admirable candour. As she shared her innermost thoughts her face began to change. The sadness began to lift a little. It wasn't that I'd said anything profound to her – it was the fact that we were sharing our pain with each other that was helping. It was human contact; a connection.

I talked about Val and how she had helped me to begin living again. I suggested that, even though it was probably the last thing on her mind, she could well meet somebody in the future.

'Not at my age,' she said wistfully.

'Well, I'm older than you!' I replied, and we both smiled a little.

It was time for a cup of tea at the Beachy Head pub. We listened to each other some more and eventually bid farewell. I can only hope that lovely woman found her way through her grief and went on to embrace life again.

Through losing Maggie and hearing so many people's stories up at Beachy Head, I've learned to value life more. People often say, 'Each day could be your last', yet carry on living as if they will be here forever. When you lose someone, and hear about other people's losses, you *really* begin to feel that way – the phrase takes on a whole new meaning. It can be terrifying, and morbid, to think that today could be your last day, but it can also be liberating. Life can change so quickly and I have learned to take each day as it comes and try to enjoy it as if it is my last. After all, each day that you are miserable is another day in your life gone. You can't get that day back, you're another day older. Obviously, I'm still susceptible to the same everyday stresses as everyone else. Money, work, traffic jams – you name it! – will always be a pain. Yet whatever is happening, I think it is vital to try and make space within each 24 hours to simply be happy and grateful for life. Find something to smile about, make yourself laugh, phone a friend just for the sake of it. Life is too precious to allow yourself to be swallowed up and made unhappy by petty matters.

Through my work at Beachy Head, I've learned not to be shy about giving people advice. I'm careful not to be pushy, but my advice is free and people can choose to take it or leave it. At the same time, I've learned to listen to people better than I could before. Really taking people's troubles on board was the only way I had a hope of saving them. In order to make sure I was doing as good a job as possible, I decided to enrol on a counselling course.

It was a very moving process. We worked in groups, and as we practised counselling each other we had to do a lot of soul searching. I already felt I was doing a good job of listening to people up at the edge, but the course armed me with even more techniques for talking and listening. I learned about body language, throwing people's words back at them and simply how to let people talk without interruption. And everything I learned, I put into practice. The course lasted three months, part time, and when I finished I walked away with a certificate to say I'd passed a person-centred counselling course. It didn't mean I was fully-trained, but at least I now possessed basic skills in counselling.

I considered taking it further and going on to be a professional counsellor, but I decided that my work at Beachy Head was too important. I knew I could do what I was already doing, so I decided to stick at it.

CHAPTER 15

WHY ARE YOU
UP HERE?

From his body language it was obvious he was very wary of me. Perhaps he was even suspicious. After all, a man who goes around making conversation with people up at a cliff edge is a little out of the ordinary, especially if he begins the conversation in a very ordinary way...

It was early in the morning. A misty, damp day and extremely wet underfoot. I had spotted a very well-built, tall man in his mid-30s, wandering along the cliff edge dressed in a very smart overcoat. Underneath, I could see he was wearing a tie. I didn't recognise him as a local walker – in fact, he looked like he would have been more at home in an office than at Beachy Head.

He seemed slightly shocked when I began talking. I opened by commenting on what a peaceful place Beachy Head is.

'But it's not without its sadness, is it?' he replied. 'It's all about death up here.'

'That's a strange thing to say, isn't it? There's also a lot of happiness up here – about a million people come here each year...'

'Well,' he said slightly defensively, 'a lot of people die up here, don't they?'

'Around 20 a year on average, yes. I lost my wife here. So, yes, you do get some unhappy people at Beachy Head.'

'Tell me about it,' he said, a hint of exasperation in his voice.

I asked him if he was happy. He wasn't.

'Is it family?' I asked.

'I don't know if I want to talk to you about it,' he said sharply. He must have felt I was being nosy, intrusive. He eyed me suspiciously and backed off.

'You don't have to talk to me. I'm only trying to be helpful,' I said. He seemed like a matter-of-fact person, so I talked to him in a matter-of-fact manner. 'I'm not going to try and force you to talk to me, but I'm here if you want to.'

'Why are you up here?' he asked. He wasn't being aggressive, but his voice was strained, his tone high-pitched. He seemed irritated and unsure of my intentions.

I explained why I was up there.

'So you're trying to stop people, are you?' he said. His manner was still a touch confrontational. He looked uneasy, as if he wasn't sure whether I was telling the truth. He began to interrogate me, questioning everything I was about. I calmly answered his questions. I knew he needed to trust me.

'It's quite simple.' I said at one point. 'If I thought you were going to try and commit suicide I would do my level best to stop you.'

Eventually, he seemed satisfied that I was for real. His tone of voice changed again and he began to open up. His wife had kicked him out. Their relationship had always been volatile, filled with arguments and fights. But it had never been physical, just verbal. Despite the fact that there had been difficulties, he desperately wanted to be with his wife. She wasn't having any of it, though. No matter what he did, she wouldn't have him back.

'Listen, mate,' I said: 'Women *do* get to the end of their tether in the end. There's a limit to how far you can push them. Are you big enough and honest enough to be able to tell me who's really at fault? Is it her who's caused the problems, or you?'

He paused thoughtfully for a moment before speaking. 'It's me,' he admitted. 'I can't keep my mouth shut. I can't hold my tongue and I flip over the smallest of things. In many ways, I've led my wife a dog's life.'

Sometimes it takes a lot to be honest with yourself, and it was obviously hard for this man to say what he'd said. I had a lot of respect for his frankness.

'Then I can understand why she doesn't want you around,' I replied, with equal candour. He may have been surprised at my forthrightness – after all, he might have expected me to tell him it was all OK – but from the way he looked at me I could tell he appreciated my honesty. I had something positive to add, though.

'You've had two children during your marriage. You've been together for a while – something must have been right at some point. All you need to do is rediscover what made you both happy and remember why you loved each other in the first place.'

I don't believe that all relationships are meant to be, but at the same time I think they often go wrong because of the stresses of life and because it can be easy to let small problems escalate and get out of hand. All marriages require work, but it's important not to lose sight of what made you love each other in the first place. And when it comes to major disagreements, it's often good to examine yourself carefully and be prepared to admit if you're in the wrong. A little bit of pride swallowing can never hurt.'

The man had been begging his wife to take him back, but he hadn't been talking about their problems. He just wanted to her to have him back again.

'You've got to give her breathing space,' I reasoned. 'If you really love her, admit to her that you're aware that you have the problem and tell her that you're prepared to work at it constructively. Tell her you're seriously committed to sorting yourself out so that you can be a better husband and give her some time. You never know, if she has time alone she may realise that she's missing your love. If you go hurtling back in, she won't have had time to trust you. Take it slowly. She needs you to prove you can change.'

The man said he'd never thought about things in that way and agreed to give it a try. He also agreed to walk away from the cliff with me.

He spoke to his wife on his mobile phone as we stood by his Jaguar in the car park. He told her he knew he was in the wrong, that he wanted to give her space, that he loved her and desperately wanted to work things out.

'What did she say?' I asked as he hung up.

'She said, "We'll see",' he replied, a little glumly.

'Well, she didn't say "No",' I countered. 'You mustn't expect too much too soon. You've hurt her a lot so try to be calm about it. Patience is everything. If you do what you say you're going to do then there's every chance she'll come back.'

He looked at me and I could see some hope had been restored in him.

'Thanks, mate,' he said, smiling. 'I'm bloody glad I met you up here.'

It was my pleasure. Sometimes men can be very hard to talk to. Despite all the turmoil this man was in, and the fact that he had started out with a very stiff upper lip, there was a way to get through to him in the end. By questioning me, he had been masking his own feelings. By the time we said goodbye, we had arrived at a point of honesty that I think he found refreshing. I certainly did.

★　　　★　　　★

Whenever I talked to people who'd been driven to the edge by marital issues, I would naturally reflect on my own marriage and thank my lucky stars that Val and I have such a solid relationship. In the first year of our marriage, we'd gone from strength to strength. I could hardly believe how wonderful everything continued to be. It was as if we were both blessed.

We've always been strong together, and it's that strength which helped us get through something that threatened to destroy Val's confidence. When I'd first met Val, she had been completely honest about something that I haven't touched on until now.

'I'll tell you this straight away,' she said, 'because when I mention it to most men, they run a mile. I've got Parkinson's Disease.'

Evidently she'd expected me to be shocked, scared and put off. I was slightly surprised that she had it, but only because hearing that anyone has such an illness is always a bit of a shock.

'Your point being?' I replied, right away. 'You and I are an item. If I told you I had cancer, would you walk away?'

'Of course I wouldn't!' she answered.

'Well, I close my case…'

The reason I haven't mentioned Val's condition until now is that it had no bearing on the way we fell in love, on whether or not we got married, nor on how much of a wonderful time we had. Put simply, Parkinson's did not stop Val and me carrying on like any normal couple.

Val's ability to be philosophical about it only made me love and admire her even more. I've heard people say to her, 'Don't you think, Why me?' Her response was always, 'Why *not* me? Who am I to say that I'm more special than anyone else?'

Val is an incredibly strong person and there was no way she was going to feel sorry for herself, or let Parkinson's get in the way of her life. At least, not as long as there was anything she could do about it. She was on a low-dosage medication and this allowed her to continue doing the things she loves. She's sport mad and a true athlete – she adores tennis, swimming, windsurfing and skiing – and kept all of them up with characteristic passion.

One day, Val began to notice a pain in the back her knee during exercise which developed into what's known as a Baker's Cyst, a condition in which you experience a bulge and a feeling of tightness behind your knee. The pain gets worse when you fully extend your knee or when you're active. The doctor told us that it was the result of a problem with Val's knee joint and that it could be arthritis. X-rays proved inconclusive, so we were told that the only way to investigate the problem was to perform keyhole surgery. We were advised that the procedure would take 15 minutes. There were hardly any risks involved, but the surgeon did mention that there was a million-to-one chance the operation could lead to Compartment Syndrome, an acute problem in which increased pressure caused by inflammation within a confined space in the body – a 'fascial compartment' – leads to impaired blood supply to the area. If Compartment Syndrome isn't treated immediately, it can lead to nerve damage and muscle death. The surgeon told us that in all the years he had been practising medicine, he had only come across the condition once. Knowing the risks, Val agreed to the surgery.

'You'll be operated on in the morning and out by the afternoon,' she was told.

The operation was in January 2007. Ken Ross is a wonderful and very experienced surgeon, but I was devastated when he called me to tell me that Val was still in surgery. The cyst had burst and the blood supply to a certain area of Val's leg had been cut off. Now Val had Compartment Syndrome. Our worst nightmare had come true.

Val had been hugely unlucky to have her operation go wrong, but she was very fortunate that such an experienced doctor was working on her. Compartment Syndrome needs to be treated immediately, and a junior or less experienced medic may not have responded to what was happening until it was too late. If Mr Ross hadn't acted so quickly and effectively, she may have had to face a leg amputation. This would be devastating for anyone but, given how active she is, it would have destroyed Val. Worse still, if left for even longer, she could have died as the blood supply to her brain could have been cut off. It doesn't bear thinking about.

Fortunately, Mr Ross acted swiftly, making a 12-inch incision to Val's leg and relieving the pressure. Her leg swelled up to nearly twice its normal size, though, and it remains very swollen to this day.

It turned out that the initial problem was arthritis and now Val had a painful, swollen leg to contend with. Suddenly she couldn't do the things she loved any more. In a matter of days, she had been reduced from someone who could do anything physically to being virtually inactive.

It was a very depressing situation; even Val found it hard to keep positive. She'd always been so strong and practical about her Parkinson's, but now she began to say negative things that were most unlike her. 'I've already got Parkinson's,' she said, 'I don't deserve this.' It was all incredibly frustrating for her. People would try to look on the bright side and tell her that she was lucky in some ways because she could have lost her leg. This was true, but Val still felt unlucky. Understandably, combined with the Parkinson's, her leg problem had made her feel terrible.

She began to lose her confidence a little, but our love for one another got us through. Despite what was happening, and the fact that Val's Parkinson's was beginning to deteriorate a bit, we were always careful to remember that we were alive and lucky to have each other.

There would be more trouble ahead, but for the moment

we learned to accept what had happened and adjust our lives accordingly. There was no point in dwelling on problems when we still had so much to live for.

★ ★ ★

The ground was soaking wet at Beachy Head. It was early in the morning and I was standing next to a man. He was wearing slippers. I didn't need to ask any questions to work out that there was something wrong.

He was about 45 years old, unshaven and quite rough looking, but very well spoken. He looked very down on his luck, but told me he didn't know exactly why he was up there.

'I'm just very pissed off,' he said grimly. 'Life is shit.'

I asked him if he wanted to talk about it.

'No!' he said emphatically, 'I do not want to talk about it. I've talked and talked to so many bloody people about it and it doesn't make a difference. I'm just fucking pissed off and that's it.'

There wasn't an awful lot I could say to that. He was adamant that he didn't want to speak and I got the impression he didn't want to listen either. Nevertheless, I stuck by him, just in case he changed his mind. I'd identified him as a 'Category Three' – I didn't think he was going to jump, but I thought he needed some TLC. For a few moments, I wasn't quite sure how to proceed. After brooding for some time, he finally spoke.

'Do you know what I could do with right now?' he asked me. 'A fag! I haven't got any money and I haven't got any fags.'

If fags were what he needed to get him down from the edge, then fags he would get. Simple, I thought. I offered to drive him into Eastbourne and buy him some. I was glad when he agreed because my early morning shift was about to finish and the chaplains were due to begin their patrol. I didn't want them, or the police, to become involved. Quite simply, I thought that this guy didn't need the potential hassle of being picked up and taken to a chapel or a police station.

He was very grateful for the cigarettes and instantly became more animated after lighting up.

'Don't even think about it,' I said, smiling. 'Just be on your way.'

Then he made a strange request. Casually, he asked me if I would drive him back up to Beachy Head!

'No I won't,' I said, a little incredulous that he seemed to think it was a possibility. 'The reason I brought you into Eastbourne is because I wanted you away from there...'

'Well if you won't take me then I'll walk.' he said. 'You needn't worry, I'm not going to kill myself. I only want to smoke my fags and enjoy the place. It's peaceful up there – a good place to think.'

Maybe he's telling the truth, I thought. And if he's going to walk back anyway, then I may as well take him. I made him promise that he would be safe. People had told me plenty of lies up at that cliff and I was very wary of believing troubled people who said they were OK. He looked squarely into my eyes and promised sincerely that he did not want to die. I believed him.

'Fine,' I said. 'I'll take you back up.'

Before I let him out of the car, I asked him once more if he was going to be OK.

'Yeah, don't worry about me,' he said brightly. 'And thanks for the fags...'

It was time to go home. As I drove off I began to worry that I may have made a mistake. I didn't want to take any chances, so I decided to phone the chaplains and ask them to keep an eye on the guy wearing slippers. I told them that he'd probably just wander up and down, but that he seemed OK.

'No problem,' they said.

I bumped into the chaplains when I returned for my lunchtime shift and asked if the man was gone.

'Yes,' one of them replied. 'We had him removed by the police.'

'You *what*?' I replied, incredulously. I didn't understand.

It turned out that when they approached him, he had become a little offensive. It got up his nose when the chaplains had started to question him and he became verbally aggressive towards them. The chaplains told me they couldn't accept his behaviour and suspected his agitation meant he was unstable. So they called the police.

To many people, a uniform is a symbol of authority and officialdom. A policeman's uniform is the best example. The Chaplaincy Team too wear uniforms when patrolling. I could be wrong, but I feel that this can sometimes make people up at the Head feel they are being persecuted by an authority figure rather being talked to by an ordinary, understanding human being. Knowing that the man had been pretty irritable with me – after all, he had told me bluntly, 'I don't want to talk to *anyone*' – I easily imagined that the presence of men in uniforms would have wound him up.

Over the years, I've heard several stories of people who have gone up to Beachy Head for a bit of peace and quiet and ended up being taken away. When I heard what had happened to the man in slippers, I felt very sorry for him and was convinced that it was all down to the chaplains and the police being rather over-zealous. Moreover, I knew he would have to be interviewed and assessed by a doctor at the police station, so he wouldn't be getting much peace and quiet either. When I'd bought him his fags, I didn't think he was in need of that sort of attention.

The police didn't section him under the Mental Health Act. He was assessed and released because he wasn't considered to be a danger to himself. But that process may have taken hours. When I was there I'd had to wait nearly 14 hours before I got to see a doctor. It made me very uptight, and being kept in a cell is one of the worst things that can be done to anyone with mental health problems.

If someone is crying out for help, throwing them in a cell is going to do no good at all. It would be far more beneficial if people were taken from Beachy Head to safe houses. Sure, the doors would be locked, but the environment would be pleasant and more conducive to helping people relax and feel comfortable. At the very least, there could be some sort of custody room for the mentally ill at police stations. It is important not to make people with mental health difficulties feel like criminals. Mental illness is a complex thing and such treatment is simply not the answer.

After he was released, the man in slippers went back to Beachy Head and ended his life. I was very shocked when I found out. I hardly knew what to think. Had I made a terrible mistake in taking him back up to the cliffs? Had he deceived me in the car? Was he going to kill himself that day? Did being taken away by the police push him over the edge, or was he going to do it anyway? All of these questions rattled around my brain. As always, I was horrified to learn of someone's death, let alone someone with whom I'd spent some time. But in this case I couldn't help but think that things might have been different if he'd been left alone to smoke his fags and think through his problems. He'd told me he was very pissed off and I can only think that being forcibly removed might have pissed him off just a little more. To this day, I feel that he may have gone back down the hill in his own time.

CHAPTER 16

HELP!

Through my binoculars, I saw a man emerge from the bushes around 50 yd from the cliff edge. My first thought was that he'd just been for a pee but I carried on watching him. He didn't move for a while, then disappeared back into the bushes. Perhaps he's a pervert, I thought to myself, and waited.

He came out again and paced to the cliff edge and back. Then he walked to the cliff edge again, and so it carried on. I started to sense that I might have a problem on my hands.

By the time I got to him, he was at the edge. He was a big guy in his forties, wore glasses and was smartly dressed in a vivid blue jumper and a jacket

'Hello, mate,' I said warmly. 'Everything all right?'

Immediately, he became aggressive. 'Yeah,' he snapped defensively. 'Why shouldn't it be?'

I was used to aggression, and had learned that the best response was to be courteous. 'Forgive me for intruding,' I began, 'but I patrol these cliffs and look out for people who may be in trouble. We get a lot of strange things happening up here, and I just wanted to check you were OK.'

'I'm just here for a walk!' he replied loudly. His face was contorted with agitation.

It was time for straight talking. I asked him if he thought it was normal to be striding repeatedly from the bushes to the cliff and back. I added that I didn't think it was and that I thought he had a problem.

'My problems are none of your bloody business!' he shouted back.

'You're right,' I replied. 'But my business is patrolling and I try to save as many people as I can. If you've got a problem, I think I can help you. All you need to do is talk and I will listen. We can get you away from here and make you safe. Are you married?'

'Yes, but what's it got to do with you?'

'Well, your wife may be very concerned about…'

'…My wife knows I'm up here!'

I asked him if she knew exactly what he was doing.

'Of course not!' he shouted, 'But she knows I'm up here walking.'

'But you're not walking. Walkers go up and down the hill,

not backwards and forwards at the top of it. I know there's a problem and if you admit that much then maybe we can find a solution for you. There's always help out there…'

His aggression began to wane. Almost begrudgingly he calmed down and began to talk a little more reasonably. Great, I thought, at least I've got him talking. He'd had problems with depression for years. It had stopped him working and he was going through a very bad patch at the moment. His wife knew all about his state of mind.

'So you're considering suicide?' I asked.

'Well, I was until you intervened,' he said.

'I don't think you really want to do it,' I said. I wanted to be as candid as possible with him. I had a gut feeling that frankness would be the key to getting this one down to safety. 'From my experience, I reckon that if you really wanted to go you would have gone before I arrived. After all, you saw me coming towards you – you had time.'

He didn't say anything. Perhaps I'd struck a chord. He looked at me expectantly. 'Perhaps we could get you some help,' I suggested. 'Why don't you come down to my car and let me call your doctor? We could call your wife too. She would understand, surely…'

'She's at work, and I can't tell her. Anyway, I've got to meet her for lunch,' he said.

'If you're planning on meeting her for lunch, then I don't think you really mean to do this, do you?' I said. My tone was kind and a little jovial, as by now I felt we'd established a good connection. I was wrong – suddenly he became aggressive again. I think he felt I was trying to catch him out.

I was quick to apologize. I told him I hadn't meant to be critical – far from it. I was trying to be compassionate. But it didn't wash. He moved to get closer to the edge. Swiftly I moved to stop him. Suddenly I realised I was all that stood between him and a 400 ft drop – and he was much bigger than me.

'Get out of my bloody way!' he yelled.

'No!' I shouted resolutely. 'You're big enough and strong enough to take me with you so, if you want to go, go! But I'll be coming with you, because I'm not going to move.'

'Don't be a bloody fool,' he sneered. 'You don't want to die, do you?'

I didn't, but I was there, my adrenaline was pumping and there was no way I could stand back and watch him jump. Nevertheless, I was scared. Compared to me, he was massive. If he was determined to die, then I was in trouble.

We were right at the edge. A couple of steps back and I'd be a goner.

The man began to try and dodge me. He shuffled to the left, and I shuffled with him. He shuffled to the right, and I moved with him. Whatever he did, there was no way he was getting past without pushing me. It was obvious he didn't want to do that – he may have been suicidal, but I didn't think he was a murderer! Much to his annoyance, I was frustrating his every effort.

'Fuck off out of here, will you!' he yelled.

All I could do was tell him to try and calm down. There was a solution to his problems, and this wasn't it. I needed assistance. Our stand-off was showing no signs of ending and I was scared about what might happen. There were other people up on the hill and I prayed that one of them would look up and clock what was going on at the edge. I was beginning to get exhausted – I felt like we'd been at it for hours. Just as I was starting to despair, the man began to calm down again. Suddenly he put his hands in his pockets and wandered away from the edge.

Now was my chance. I'd been desperate to call for help but there was no way that I could have risked taking my phone out while I'd been between the man and thin air. I reached into my pocket to get my phone.

'What the fuck are you doing?' screamed the man.

'Don't worry,' I said, 'I've just got to text my wife to tell her I've been delayed. I'm not phoning the police. I'll show you her message when she writes back.' To my relief, he seemed happy with this and calmed down again.

I'd send Val the message while talking to him. It comprised only one word: 'HELP!' God knows what I would have done if he'd asked to see my outgoing message. Luckily, he was satisfied by Val's one word reply – 'OK.'

Val phoned the police and told them I was in trouble up at Beachy Head. She didn't know what was wrong, but she knew I needed them. She also asked them not to go up with their sirens wailing – I'd told her in the past that it would spook whoever I was struggling with.

The police asked Val where I was and she told them that she only knew I was somewhere at Beachy Head. They insisted on ringing me, but Val knew that this could also spook the person I was with and refused to give them my number. She told them to stop wasting time and just get up there. But they didn't listen. They insisted on having my number. Their procedure is such that they said they couldn't do anything without it. In the end, Val gave in. Sure enough, the police called me straight away.

The man glared at me as my phone rang. He was wide-eyed and suspicious. I had to think fast. I had no choice but to answer it. 'Oh hello, how are you?' I said, casually. I had decided to bluff in order to try and convince the man that I was chatting with a mate. The police asked me where I was. 'Yeah, be great to see you soon,' I said. 'Sometime next week, maybe. It's a lovely day up here at Belle Toute. I love Beachy Head.'

At last, the police were on their way. I was relieved yet at the same time petrified that they would have their sirens and lights on. If they do, I thought, the man might panic, make a lunge for it and take me with him.

Minutes later, I heard the sound of sirens. Shit, I thought, I just knew it! I prepared myself for the worst. If the man was going to go for it, now was the time. But he didn't. Instead, he suddenly turned away and began to saunter down the hill as if he didn't have a care in the world. I could hardly believe my luck.

'Where are you going?' I asked incredulously. He told me he was going back to his car. 'Hang on,' I said, 'I'll come with you.' I didn't want to take any chances – there was always a chance he was calling my bluff. Judging from his erratic behaviour so far, I half expected him to turn at any moment and start running back up the hill.

By the time the police had legged it up to us, we were halfway down the hill.

'Hello sir,' said an officer. 'How are you?

'Fine thanks,' said the man breezily. I was a little gobsmacked, I must say.

'Well, it's been suggested to us that you may be about to commit suicide,' replied the officer.

'No, I'm just out for a walk.' He was completely nonchalant about everything. I could hardly tell which was more farcical – the last hour of playing cat and mouse, or this.

One officer walked down to the man's car with me while I filled him in on the details. Another went off and had a chat with the man and a policeman. I couldn't hear what they were saying but after about five minutes the officer came over to me to tell me everything was OK. There was no problem here.

'I beg your pardon?' I said in disbelief. I was told that the police reckoned the man was fine. I was astounded.

'So I've just spent an hour with a man trying to dodge me

at the edge of a cliff and you're telling me there's nothing wrong with him?' It felt laughable.

The police felt that he was fine because he hadn't talked about wanting to kill himself. It was the man's word against mine. I was worried that he might go back up, but unfortunately there was nothing more that could be done.

Suddenly, things took an even more surreal turn. The man I'd just been trying to save now approached me – and asked me if I was OK!

'Yes,' I replied, 'what about you?'

'I'm fine, thanks,' he said, before turning to all of us. 'Can I offer any of you gentlemen a lift?'

All of our cars were in the other car park, and before I knew it the two police officers and I were being driven back by this rather strange individual. I kept on shaking my head with disbelief. It was truly bizarre.

'Bye-bye everybody,' chirped the man after we'd got out of the car. It was almost funny, but I was still very concerned about him.

'I can't believe you just let him go,' I said to the cops. 'You should go after him, at least.' The police did follow him for a while, but nothing came of it.

I was glad that he was safe, but I was also reeling a bit from the whole episode. The police were very appreciative of my efforts, though, and apologised that they were unable to do more. The law is the law and they couldn't detain or question him further if he told them everything was fine.

Since that crazy day, I've seen the man in Eastbourne a few times. He always waves hello to me and I wave back. To this day I cannot decide if his behaviour was merely a bizarre charade, or whether he would have jumped if I hadn't been there. All I know is that he kept trying to run past me to get to the edge, and that is worrying behaviour. Perhaps he just has an oddly developed sense of humour and was winding me up.

I'm so glad he's still alive and I'm glad he waves to me, but I'll never forget the massive mood swings he displayed. From minute to minute he veered from being high and aggressive to low and depressive, agitated in one breath and waving goodbye the next. I worry that he is another Bella – that he threw us off the scent but that one day he will do it. I hope to God that I never read about him in the paper.

CHAPTER 17

FACING THE
MUSIC

A car sped towards mine and whizzed past. I pulled over
and watched it career up the hill before it turned
around and came back again. It came to a stop in a bus
turnaround point. Two girls leapt out and began talking to
each other animatedly. They were gesticulating wildly, as if
something was desperately wrong. Concerned by now, I
joined them.

The girls were in their late teens and very distressed. 'We're
looking for our brother,' one of them told me, quite
hysterically. 'We know he's in a bit of a state and have a
feeling that he might be up here.'

I told them what I did and asked them to follow me on
foot. The best place to start was up at the most popular
jumping spot – the highest point of Beachy Head. We

mounted the hill and, sure enough, there was a well-built, mousey-haired boy sitting on the cliff edge.

His sisters wanted to approach him, but I wasn't sure if it was a good idea. If someone is suicidal, being faced with hysterical emotion from family isn't always the best way to convince them to think again.

'I do this a lot,' I told them, as kindly as I could. 'My advice is to let me deal with it for a few minutes. Do you mind?'

They agreed to stay about 30 yards back. I approached the boy slowly, and sat down carefully nearby. I had a feeling that he wasn't about to go, so I started off slowly.

'You've got two young ladies looking for you, you know,' I said softly.

He knew that, he said, so I asked him what the problem was. The problem was his family. He was very unhappy indeed. He'd always been the black sheep, he'd been trodden on; he felt like the world was against him and he wanted out. It's always terrible to hear someone so young saying such dark things when they have so much to live for. He told me he was good for nothing and a tear fell from his eye.

'You must be good at *something*,' I said consolingly, cheerily. 'Everyone's got some kind of skill.'

He shook his head a little and shrugged. I didn't want to push him, so I waited for him to talk next.

'Well, I do write songs,' he said hesitantly.

'There you go!' I enthused. 'That's a skill in itself! *I*

couldn't write two words, let alone a song. You should be proud of what you can do...'

He didn't seem too buoyed up by my words. In fact, he looked dejected! 'Nobody wants to know about my songs – nobody reads my words, nobody ever wants to listen,' he said through his tears. He seemed inconsolable, but I found it hard to believe that no one was interested.

'Well, have you actually tried to get people to listen to them?' I asked.

The boy paused and looked at me. No, he admitted, he hadn't. There was a folder by his side. It contained his song lyrics. Sheepishly, hopefully, the boy asked me if I'd like to read some of them. Needless to say, I told him I'd be thrilled.

He handed me the folder. Five minutes must have gone by before I said anything, because from the moment I began to read I was completely absorbed by this boy's work – his lyrics were staggeringly good! I could hardly believe that a boy so young had come up with such powerful and mature work.

I read around ten songs before I looked up. The boy was looking at me nervously, expectantly. Even if his lyrics had been terrible, I would have told him they were good, but there was no need for me to search for kind words. The praise just tumbled out of my mouth.

'These are absolutely *brilliant!*' I began. His face brightened just a little.

'But they're not that good really, are they?' he asked, cautiously. Perhaps he thought I was just being nice. I didn't hesitate to reassure him that they were really, *really* good. I was so enthusiastic that he had no choice but to accept my compliments! Only now did he begin to look a touch cheerier.

'One thing I noticed,' I commented, 'is that they are all very sad…' The words were brilliant for sure, but all pretty mournful.

'I write like that because that's how I feel,' he said frankly. Fair enough, I thought, but I wanted to tell him about my story in the hope that he may come to believe that life wasn't all doom and gloom.

He listened attentively to me as I told him Maggie's story. He showed interest in the way that I had turned a negative into a positive, and he was particularly drawn in by my suggestions for how he could get people to listen to his music.

'It doesn't matter that these songs are sad,' I said. 'What matters is that it's making you sad that no one wants to hear them. Well, I can tell you that a lot of people take comfort from sad songs and getting your work heard will make you happy. 'You've got to use that sadness to your advantage…'

He nodded as I spoke, but told me that he didn't think anyone would listen, most of all his parents. In fact, it turned out that he'd barely tried to get his parents to listen – he'd just assumed that they wouldn't want to. I told him to try and if he failed then to try someone else. There would be an audience for his music if he looked for it, but it wasn't going to come to him.

'Get out there,' I encouraged him. 'Go to London, put your music on the internet, send out demos. With lyrics like these, you'll have an audience before you know it!' My advice was simple – obvious, even – but it seemed to do the trick. By the time I'd finished, he seemed inspired to take the reins and try concertedly to make himself heard.

Then came the best bit. He stood up and back from the edge, turned around and began to walk down the hill. Up until now he hadn't realised that the girls were waiting for him, but he didn't mind. One of the two was his girlfriend – he took her in his arms and held her tight. All seemed well.

But there was one problem. The boy's sister had phoned their parents and they were on their way to pick him up. When the boy found out, he was far from pleased. He began to shout that he didn't want to see them, that he *couldn't* see them. Oh God, I thought, He's going to go back up the cliff. No sooner had I started to be on my guard again than a car pulled into the car park. It was his parents.

The boy froze as they got out and began to walk towards us.

They hugged him together.

'Come on, son, let's go home,' said his father, before turning to thank me for everything. I was relieved as I watched them walk back to the car – but my happiness was short-lived.

Almost as soon as the car doors were shut, a huge row broke out. I wasn't close enough to hear what was being said, but it didn't matter. The noise and the body language of all concerned was enough – this was no reconciliation! The next thing I knew, the boy had jumped out of the car, slammed the door and begun to stride angrily up the hill. I ran to catch up with him.

'I told you, didn't I?' he shouted through tears, 'They're not bloody listening to me. They don't want to know about my music. All they want to do is criticise.'

I put my arm around him, terrified he was going to make a run for it. He was becoming hysterically upset. I had to calm him down, and quick. I begged him not to do anything rash and asked him to give me a chance to talk to his parents. He agreed to stay put while I went to have a word.

His parents were distraught that their son was in such a state, though they felt they couldn't understand him or get close to him. They were surprised to find out how much their son's songs meant to him – they simply didn't realise how central his music was to his existence. I told them what an intelligent, talented young man they had brought up, and I added that if they wanted to understand their boy they could do nothing better than read his songs. To understand his lyrics would be to understand the place he was in mentally. I said that I thought he was vulnerable and may need some help, but added that there's nothing like the understanding and love of a family to keep someone from sinking into depression.

The boy came back down and they all hugged once more.

There was a lot of talking and listening to be done, but from the looks on all of their faces I could tell that it was going to happen. When they got back into the car, I sensed a calmness and acceptance in his parents' eyes that hadn't been there when they had first arrived. I knew all the boy needed was to feel recognised and accepted for who and what he was, and as I watched them talking calmly to each other it was plain that the boy was speaking from the heart. It was also plain that his parents had begun to appreciate the importance of really listening.

They're going to get through this, I thought. I could feel it in my heart – which is just where that boy felt his music.

CHAPTER 18

YOU'RE REALLY
PISSING US OFF

It was May 2007. I was up at Beachy Head, filming for a
TV piece about my work. The TV company wanted to
interview both the chaplains and myself in order to get a
rounded perspective, but the chaplains had refused to
comment. What happened next really hammered home to
me exactly how some of them felt about my presence up at
the cliffs.

The camera crew were finishing the day's filming up by
taking a few scenic shots of Beachy Head as the sun began
to drop. As the camera panned across the cliffs, two chaplains
came into the picture. While they had refused to be
interviewed, nothing had been said about the filming itself
and we knew we had the right to film whatever we wanted
– Beachy Head is common land, after all. The camera kept
rolling – it was great, atmospheric footage.

I recognised one of the chaplains – our relationship had always been courteous and we had got on reasonably well. Little did I know this was all about to change. He noticed that we were filming, stopped walking and glared at me for a second or two before calling out three words I will never forget.

'Keith! Here! Now!' I hadn't been spoken to like that since my schooldays. I looked at the cameraman, who was as shocked as me. Perhaps we hadn't heard right, I thought.

'I beg you pardon?' I called back.

'Come here now!' he shouted.

I wondered if they needed my help looking for someone, so began to walk over with a cameraman and a female journalist in tow.

'You two stay where you are!' shouted the chaplain. 'I only want Keith!'

I continued walking. 'Hello there, what's up?' I said. 'Do you need some help?'

He looked at me with anger and contempt and I guessed that help was not what he was after. 'You're really pissing me off now,' he said venomously. 'You truly piss us all off!'

'*Pardon?*' I said. 'That's not very Christian, is it?'

The chaplain gave no answer. He turned on his heel and stormed off. I was flabbergasted and as I turned around to the cameraman and the journalist I noticed they were laughing.

'What are you giggling at?' I said.

'You're still miked up,' they replied. 'We heard every word and it's on tape!'

Before we had a chance to laugh too much, another chaplain had stormed up to me. He shouted for us to turn the camera off and then began to have a go at me.

'You know how we feel about publicity...' he began, but I wasn't interested in listening to a rant.

'I don't court publicity,' I cut in, 'and I also don't expect to be sworn at by you lot.'

He denied there had been swearing, but soon backed down when I pointed out that everything that had been said was on tape. The machines were off now, though, so he didn't hold back from continuing to give me a piece of his mind.

'You know you cause deaths up here, don't you?' he said.

'You *what*?' I said. 'Don't you dare say that to me!' I was disgusted by his accusation. It was hard to believe someone was being so offensive to my face. There was nothing more to say. After staring at me for a few moments, the chaplain turned and walked away.

'I think we've seen enough,' said the journalist. 'It's quite clear what you're dealing with up here.'

I think they were more shocked than I about the behaviour of the chaplains. I'd grown used to the idea that I was no longer wanted, but to outsiders such an attitude appeared very offensive indeed. I asked them to destroy the tape, as I didn't want to make the chaplains look bad on TV, but they refused, telling me that the material on it was a journalist's dream. They didn't use it for a programme in the end, but they still have it. 'Don't worry Keith,' the journalist had told me. 'We've got the tape should you ever need it!

I don't believe the publicity I received harmed anyone. Used in the right way, publicity can only help address a problem, and my interviews were always conducted in order to make the public aware of the problem of suicide, and to encourage the council to do more about it. When facing a problem in life, you can do two things: you can face up to the issue or you can bury your head in the sand and hope it will go away. I think that, to a certain extent, the chaplains, the coastguards and the council are burying their heads in the sand about the problem of suicide at Beachy Head. I also think that by accusing me of contributing to it, certain people were looking for a scapegoat.

The number of deaths at Beachy Head fell between 2004 and 2006. In 2004 there were 34 deaths, while in 2005 there were 26 and 7 in 2006, so I can safely say that my presence did not make things worse during that period. Perhaps it made things better – I wouldn't like to say. Figures began to rise again after that, but I don't think it had anything to do with me. In truth, my publicity is a drop in the ocean when compared the amount of publicity Beachy Head gets in general. One only need to go on a suicide website (and there is a depressingly large number of them) to find directions to and information about Beachy Head. Suicide at Beachy Head has been around a lot longer than I have, and now I have stopped my patrols the figures are rising again. Not that

I think my absence has anything to do with that. One man alone could not govern how many people kill themselves. Rather, it is the pressures of life – especially money and the economy – that tend to affect suicide rates.

The problem with Beachy Head isn't publicity – it's down to depression and people wanting to die as a result of it. Depression and suicide are subjects that people bury their heads in sand about too. Suicide is one of the biggest killers in this country and I wanted to draw attention to that. Prevention is better than cure, and in my interviews I always tried to raise public awareness about depression in the hope that those suffering from it would feel that there was hope and would seek help and understanding.

★   ★   ★

Around this time, Val and I had some good news and some bad news. The bad news came first. Val had been taking a relatively new wonder drug for her Parkinson's – and indeed, it had been working wonders for her. Parkinson's disease is a degenerative disorder of the central nervous system that impairs the sufferer's motor skills. As the disease progresses, the symptoms worsen and it is very common for a person to experience uncontrollable tremors, or shaking. Val's medication had virtually eliminated her tremors, along with other symptoms. Everything seemed completely under control. And then, in May 2007, a bomb was dropped on us. We were told that one of her drugs may have caused her heart damage. It was a remote possibility, but it was worth having a heart scan for peace of mind.

We tried not to think the worst and Val went for the scan. A few weeks later we were called back, and were told that it had revealed damage to two of the valves in Val's heart. It was a massive shock. When the doctor told us the bad news we simply sat there, mouths agape. First there had been the one-in-a-million disaster with her leg and now we were being told that, very unluckily, she had heart damage. After a few moments of shock, Val simply broke down. It was all too much to take on board.

They needed to do more tests to find out how bad the damage was. 'Who knows,' the doctor said. 'You may get over this. We'll change your drugs, and your heart may even heal itself. In the meantime, you must do everything in moderation to avoid placing stress on your heart…'

What did he mean? Was he saying that Val might die if she didn't take it easy? How were we to gauge moderation? How long is a piece of string?

Three months later, there were more tests… and it turned out that Val's heart wasn't going to heal itself after all. In fact, the damage was getting worse. The only option was open-heart surgery – and she needed it within two years. The operation itself carries several risks and the recovery period can be long and painful. Combined with Val's Parkinson's, and the ongoing problem of the Compartment Syndrome, it felt like an ongoing nightmare.

I saw Val's strength begin to waver a little; it was painful to witness such a strong, vibrant woman being crushed by something else that was beyond her control. And to think that all this was due to the medication she had been taking to help her with Parkinson's – it felt like a sick joke.

Understandably, Val became a little depressed about life. Naturally, she felt it was unfair that she had three major physical problems when plenty of people her age had none. She didn't wish her problems on anyone else, but was simply devastated that she had so much to cope with.

Until now, we'd been on a blissful high – meeting, falling in love, getting married and going around the world – and now we had come crashing down to earth. The bottom line was that we were petrified of losing each other and the thought of being without Val was tearing me to pieces.

A terrible dread began to build inside me. I'd lost Maggie. Was history about to repeat itself? After all, it had already done so in a number of ways:

I met Maggie in a pub. I met Val in a pub.

Maggie was blonde. Val too.

I proposed to Maggie in Paris. I did the same with Val.

I had been on a massive high with Maggie and was on a massive high with Val.

Maggie's health had begun to go wrong and now so had Val's.

Maggie had died. Was I going to lose the precious woman who'd brought me back to life again? I didn't dare to dwell on what would happen if I lost Val. Instead, I focused on a subtle difference between Maggie and Val.

Even though she was ill, Maggie chose to die. She had an addictive personality, and this made it easy to succumb to drowning herself in alcohol and descending into alcoholism. Coupled with this, she had an unhappy childhood, and terrible things had happened to her throughout her life, which led to low self-esteem and depression. In some ways, I don't think Maggie was willing to acknowledge the problems she had so that she could go on to deal with them. In the end, I believe she was only fighting for my sake rather than hers, and that's what made her give up the fight. She chose to die because she felt she couldn't win the battle with her demons. I loved her but she didn't love herself enough to want to live.

Val's problems are different. They are physical. Val had a happy childhood, she doesn't suffer from depression, she recognises what is wrong with her and, above all, she wants to live. She is a fighter. When I thought about what might lay ahead, I knew there was no way she'd go down without a struggle. Maggie wanted to die, whereas Val didn't, and that gave me hope.

Whatever happened, I knew I had to be strong for Val and I knew I was up to the task. I've always been a caring person. I put that down to my wonderful parents – they gave me a fantastic upbringing, taught me right from wrong and shaped me into a polite, giving person. I was always ready to help anyone in trouble. I'd tried with Maggie and now I would try again with Val. In the coming months there would be times when I'd want to lie down and cry my eyes out with fear and worry, but I would rein myself in and be strong. At other times, I would temporarily lose my composure and break down uncontrollably in Val's arms, telling her I didn't want to lose her and that I was scared to death. But it was Val who was suffering the most. She felt vulnerable and scared of death, and it was time for me to look after her. Life was changing, but I knew we'd rise to the occasion and do everything we could to get through it. I hoped the spirits were with us, I hoped Maggie was with us and I hoped I would be able to offer Val the support she needed as we waited for the operation. It was likely to be a long wait.

I also began to wonder how long I would be able to keep patrolling up at Beachy Head. I still had to go to work to earn money, and with Val's health problems I knew that I would need to devote more and more time to caring for her. Even though I loved patrolling, my priorities would have to change eventually. Heart problems aside, I always knew that Val's Parkinson's meant that, one day, I would be caring for her full time – and naturally, I was fully prepared to do that. But for the time being, I decided I would try to keep on with my patrols. They meant so much to me, and it meant so much to Val that I didn't stop doing what I was passionate about until I needed to.

And then we received the good news. Val received some inheritance money, and, combined with generous financial help from her mother, it was enough to enable us to pay for private treatment. Instead of waiting for up to two years, we could begin to plan the operation for 2008. The money also allowed me to cut back on my working hours and keep my work at Beachy Head going while still having time free to look after Val. We'd taken some blows, but it seemed that fate was smiling a little more up on us of late.

CHAPTER 19
BANKRUPT

I was on the edge at the highest point on Beachy Head – and unfortunately, I wasn't alone. Beside me was a man with watery eyes and a sunken head. The problem? He was a businessman, but had lost everything. He didn't have a penny to his name.

He was wringing his hands up and down, shaking his head and twitching nervously inside a trench coat. I was highly anxious too. He's going to go over if I don't find the right words, I thought. I had to find them fast.

I said all I could to try and calm him down, telling him that it just wasn't worth ending one's life because of finances. 'Money makes the world go around,' I said, 'but you can't place a value on human life.'

It seemed to register with him. He stopped wringing his

hands, and shoved them into his coat pockets. At least now he was talking to me. We ended up having quite a long chat. Although he agreed with me that suicide was a desperate measure, and that money wasn't the most important thing in life, he couldn't cope with the enormity of his situation. It's all very well being poor, but not having a penny to your name and going bankrupt at the age of 40 is pretty overwhelming. He didn't know who or what to turn to. He was prepared to step away from the edge, but there was no way of walking away from his problems.

We walked down the hill, and ended up at his car – a beaten-up old Ford Fiesta. He was a smart-looking man – he looked like the type of businessman who should be driving a Mercedes or a Jaguar – and even though I was pleased he'd come back down to the car park, I felt that it would be irresponsible of me to just bid him farewell. I didn't want to see him up there again, or worse still discover he'd killed himself while I wasn't around to stop him. Looking at the despair in his eyes as we stood by his car, I decided to try and help him a little more.

Although I'd given plenty of people advice up at the cliff edge, I was no financial adviser. I could persuade him to think twice about killing himself, but I couldn't tell him how to begin to sort out his money matters. I knew he needed professional help and that's why, once I'd got him away from danger, I decided to call the chaplains.

I'm just an ordinary bloke on his own, whereas the

chaplains are an organisation with support networks that they have built up over the years. They have access to counsellors, and if someone in trouble needs a bed for the night, they can provide it. Also, they have advisors who are there to help people with financial worries.

Whatever my popularity amongst some of the chaplains, it wasn't going to stop me from getting in touch to tell them I'd found a man in need of their help. I explained everything and a chaplain came to meet the man before I left. I felt I'd done all I could and was glad that the guy was going to get some follow-up advice.

I'm not sure exactly what happened after I left, but it turned out that he ended up getting taken away by the police. I was very shocked when I discovered this, because it didn't add up. When I'd said goodbye to the bloke, he had been calm, reasonable and ready to accept any help and advice on offer. He thanked me for my help and I assured him he was in good hands.

Having spoken to others who have been talked down by the chaplains, I've often heard that part of the conversation tends to involve God. The chaplains are religious, so I suppose it follows that they might say things like 'God will help you', 'We will pray for you' and that they ask people to turn to the Almighty in their hour of need. This is all very well if the person they are talking to happen to be a Christian, but I think it could cause considerable offence to anyone who isn't. After all, if you are thinking of ending your life and you are a person of another faith – or no faith at all – you wouldn't want to hear talk of a Christian God.

The chaplains are good people with the most noble of intentions – saving lives – but I feel that they could downplay their faith a little at times. A dog-walker once said to me that if someone breaks wind up at Beachy Head, it's an incident for the chaplains. There are times when I've been over-cautious too and have approached people who are fine, but I didn't do it in a red uniform and I didn't mention God. Nonetheless, the chaplains are doing a great job, which the public should continue to support with their donations.

I was very disappointed that the bankrupted man had been removed by the police. I felt terrible for him. Perhaps he would have been better off if I'd just let him go his own way. It's hard to know. Either way, I'd arrived at a point where I decided it wasn't worth me contacting the chaplains again. Even though I had a lot of respect for what they were trying to do up at Beachy Head, we had very different methods.

*   *   *

The woman looked very depressed. It was a lovely day in late August, but she certainly wasn't enjoying it. She sat on one of the natural ledges, her head hanging down, her shoulders slumped forwards. I doubted that she was going to jump, but I needed to be sure. Anyway, it was obvious she needed some care and attention, so I sat down next to her and told her about my patrols.

'What's making you so depressed?' I enquired after a few minutes. 'Is it relationship problems?'

'No, I've got a lovely boyfriend,' she said. 'It my job.'

'Well a job can't be a reason to kill yourself, can it? What do you do?'

'I work in mental care.'

Mental care? I thought. I've had plenty of people up here who were under mental care, but never have I talked down one of the carers!

'I get so down and despondent about it,' she continued sadly. 'Sufficient facilities for patients aren't there, the funding isn't there and every time I get told that a patient needs one thing or another, I realise we're unable to offer it to them. We simply don't have enough money and it depresses the hell out of me.

'I care so much for these people and nothing is being done for them. They become ill, they're given pills and are shoved off into Care in the Community. There's much more that should be done for the mentally ill. I feel so bad because I don't think I can cope with this job any more, but I want to be helping them.' It was very moving to listen to her story.

Eventually, she walked away. She told me she knew she wasn't alone among NHS staff. Thanks to limited resources, many of her colleagues were under huge amounts of stress and suffering from depression. The fact of the matter was that they just couldn't cope with the number of people in need of help and felt terrible that what they could offer was often so limited.

I'd never been a professional carer, but I had met plenty of people up at Beachy Head who felt the NHS was failing them and I had often felt that the state of mental health services was pretty lamentable. Now I was talking to somebody from the other side of the fence and she only served to confirm my worst fears.

When Maggie was suffering from depression, I had often felt disappointed by the treatment she received from the NHS. At one point, I was convinced that she needed to be sectioned for her own safety – she was behaving in a way that made me think she was going to attempt suicide. We were told to wait in A & E, and I was shocked to see a lot of people with cuts, bruises and broken arms mixed up with people who obviously had severe mental health problems. Depressives and people suffering from schizophrenia were being told they may have to wait up to 12 hours to see someone and it just didn't seem right. There was no access to help in an emergency. People with injuries need attending to, of course, and it's frustrating for anyone to have to wait a long time to be seen. However, when there are people who feel suicidal in A & E, I feel they should be treated in the same way as anyone with a life-threatening condition and not made to wait – especially as one's state of mind in these situations can be unpredictable and the person may become increasingly desperate in a short space of time. Waiting just makes things worse.

Maggie was eventually seen, but the doctor had treated

her very dismissively. 'She's a drunk,' he'd announced. 'Sort her out!'

'All right,' I'd replied, 'I'll take her away. But if my wife kills herself tonight, I'm coming back for you!'

With that, he agreed to section her. Maggie was put in a curtained-off area on a ward, but because of her fragile mental state she felt intimidated and insecure. This wasn't helped by other patients on the ward lifting the curtain to have a look at her. I had to leave her overnight and it broke my heart when I walked out of that hospital, arrived at my car and looked up at a window to see Maggie peering down at me. She looked so vulnerable and lonely, and I didn't know what care she was going to receive. I wondered if I was doing more harm than good by leaving her in there.

I don't blame that doctor for trying to get rid of Maggie – NHS resources are so overstretched that it's little wonder he initially wanted me simply to take her back home. Maggie didn't receive much help from the NHS once she had been sectioned, and she went on to kill herself.

I don't agree with the way mental health is dealt with these days. In many ways, I think the principle of old-fashioned mental hospitals should be brought back. It makes sense to have specialist homes for people with mental difficulties, each of which would have their own equivalent to A & E; physical and mental health should be very much separated and dealt with in different ways. I believe that politicians closed down all the mental hospitals because they were costing too much and unlikely to win public support. The government like to allocate funds to things that win votes – spending money on equipment for fighting cancer and heart disease is worth boasting about, but telling the public that their money is being spent to help the mentally ill isn't going to make a political party shoot up in the polls.

Depression and mental illness is misunderstood in this country. Many people think of depression as a little bit made-up, and I think they find it hard to accept that it is a real, clinical condition that cripples the victim. If the depression gets too severe, it can lead to suicide. It is a potentially fatal illness that is no different to cancer or heart disease and the government should be doing a lot more to help those suffering from it.

Consider this. Around 2,500 people die on the Britain's roads each year, and around 5,000 people die from suicide. It is estimated that for every suicide there are around 20 people severely affected by the loss – mums and dads, husband and wives, brothers and sisters and so on – and that out of those, at least two are also likely to go on to kill themselves. Untreated, depression breeds more depression – a snowball effect. Every single person who commits suicide has fallen through the net and treating those who are victims of it only puts more pressure on the NHS. I am not blaming the NHS for every suicide, but I think that much, much more could be done to help those who are depressed and prevent such unnecessary loss of life.

The NHS has been used as a political football for so long – politicians bombard us with figures about how much money is being spent on it, and the opposition always say they would do things differently if only they could, but in my view nothing really changes. I think the only solution to the problem is to take healthcare out of the political arena. It should be run by an all-party committee of politicians, financial experts and managerial staff – much as it is now really, but the key difference would be that money could be allocated wherever it is needed. There would be no bias towards distributing resources in order to win votes, because it wouldn't be a subject that was part of a political debate – all parties would be responsible and areas such as mental health would stand more of a chance of receiving adequate funding.

I can dream, can't I? If that dream came true and resources could be properly allocated, then maybe we'd no longer find mental health carers up at Beachy Head...

CHAPTER 20

THE SHIT HITS
THE FAN

I spotted a woman's head and rushed over until I could see the rest of her. She was sitting about 8 ft below Maggie's cross, just at the point where the cliff curves away to a vertical drop. It is such a steep slope – about 70 degrees – that I could hardly believe she had managed to get so far down without slipping away. Immediately, I was petrified. There was no way I could lurch for her, no way I could pull her back. She was so precariously balanced that any movement would send her flying – and me too. More to the point, I would have to climb down to get to her. At first, all I could do was talk, and I didn't want to scare her. I started off by saying 'Hello' very, very quietly.

She turned her head very slowly and I could see she was petrified too. There was no time for explaining who I was.

'You're not thinking of jumping are you, darling?' I said softly.

'I was going to,' she said, her voice wavering, 'but I thought of my children and changed my mind. I can't get back.'

She was trapped. She may have changed her mind about dying, but whether she wanted to or not I could tell there was a good chance she was about to. I could see her bottom begin to lose its purchase on the chalk – it was leaving a little track behind her. Very slowly, she was sliding away. There was only one thing for it: I'd have to go down and try to bring her back.

'I'm going to come and get you,' I said. 'Just keep as still as you can. We need to try and stop the sliding.'

I walked down as far as I could, then sat down and began to slide myself gently down the cliff. Any sudden movement and I'd be gone. It must have taken just a couple of minutes for me to reach her, but it seemed like an eternity. 'Don't worry, sweetheart,' I said when I got to her. 'I'm with you now. Here's what I want you to do. When I tell you to, I want you to lock your arm into mine. You're not going to fall, I promise.'

That was a complete and utter lie – we were so far down that I could see the waves lapping at the shore a few hundred feet below and the chalk we were sitting on was far from stable. I could feel myself beginning to slide.

I gave her the instruction to lock arms with me, which she did. She was very nervous – almost hysterical with fear – and even though I was desperate for us to get away from the edge, I needed her to regain some composure first.

'Now, I want you to take some deep breaths and try to calm down a little,' I said, holding her tight. She did as instructed and after a minute or so she seemed to have steadied her mind a little.

'When I say go, you're going to move your left buttock up, back and down again, and then do the same with your right buttock. I'm going to do the same – it's very important that we do this together while we hold on to each other. OK?'

She nodded.

I tried to dig my heels in to the chalk, but they slipped over it; very slowly, I twisted my legs so that the sides of my shoes were pressing into it. I managed to get a tiny, yet vital grip on the cliff face, and instructed her to copy me. It was time to try and move.

'Go!' I said.

Cheek by cheek, we retreated from the edge. With every tiny movement, we advanced closer to the safety of the grass. Little by little, I began to feel a little more at ease. By the time we were clear of the chalk and I knew we weren't going to die, it felt as if half an hour had passed. In reality, our bum shuffling probably only took around five minutes, but it was one of the most intense five minutes of my life. I hauled the woman on to the grass, grabbed her arm and told her it was safe to stand up and walk.

'Well, I'm certainly glad that's over,' I sighed, smiling, once we got back to the top. We hugged each other, and I looked over her shoulder to where we had been sitting only minutes ago. It was only then that I realised exactly how much danger we'd been in. Put simply, I nearly crapped myself!

A chaplain came over to us. The woman had told me she was in financial difficulty and I hoped they would offer her some help. I was shocked at their opening words.

'What the hell do you think you're doing?' one of them shouted. 'You could have killed her!' Killed her? She was about to die, there hadn't been a moment to lose. The rant continued before I had a chance to reply. 'You should *not* have gone down there. You should have called the coastguards to save her. You could have killed her, and you could have killed yourself!'

I was truly gobsmacked. It took me a few moments to appreciate just how insane these comments were. Health and Safety rules and regulations had obviously burrowed themselves deep into this man's head. That's why he was telling me that I should have called the coastguard. The rules state that harnesses are required for anyone trying to save someone. Following the rules, though, would have meant the woman who was standing safely by my side would have been long gone by now.

'If I'd have called the coastguard it would have taken 20 minutes for them to arrive, and even longer for them to harness themselves up and make sure they were safe enough to perform the rescue. This woman had about two minutes...'

'That's no excuse. Under no circumstances should you put lives at risk!'

What bizarre logic. If I want to put my life at risk, that's my problem, I thought. 'Well, if that's your way of doing things, fine!' I shouted. 'It's not mine. I'm proud of what I've just done. I've saved a life and all you can do is wave the book at me. Well you've got a rotten, stinking problem and there's something dreadfully wrong with you!'

It's difficult to describe how livid I was. I was being accused of nearly killing a woman whom I'd just saved, and it felt like madness. Standing there with that chaplain, I wanted to grab hold of him, shake him and scream, 'Have you got any fucking common sense? Don't you think life is more important the Health and bloody Safety regulations?' What would he have done if faced with a woman who had two minutes to live? Said a little prayer for her as she slid to her death? Would he have comforted himself with the thought that God would look after her in the next life and would he have gone home happy that he hadn't broken the rules? If that was Christianity, he could stick it.

But I didn't do any of those things. I left the woman with the chaplains and walked away. There was no point in wasting my breath.

I was cross and deeply disappointed. All I've ever wanted to do at Beachy Head is save lives. I appreciate that every society needs rules, but life isn't always black and white. There are some moments when you have to buck the trend and break the rules for the sake of pure logic, to be able to get the job done. Sometimes, you have to forget about Health and Safety and put your life on the line. I didn't flout the rules for the sake of breaking them. I flouted them because I had no choice. Moreover, in my view, a rule that tells someone they can't take a risk to save someone else is a pretty dumb rule in the first place. There are good rules and there are bad ones. Some aspects of Health and Safety law make sense, while others are just a lot of twaddle.

The incident had left me feeling distraught, and as I drove home to Val I began to think that my time at Beachy Head might be about to come to an end. I'd been snubbed, sworn at and accused of contributing to suicide rates at Beachy Head. I'd been reprimanded for ignoring Health and Safety rules and now, to top it all off, just after saving someone I was being accused of nearly killing her. I didn't know how much more I could endure. I felt that despite my best efforts, despite three years of commitment and numerous saves, I was being brushed aside as a nuisance. I was exhausted.

After talking to Val about it all, I came to a decision. I wouldn't stop my patrols, but I'd cut back. I wasn't going up to Beachy Head in order to be insulted, so I decided I would only go up there when I knew I'd be alone. I would continue with my early morning patrol, but that would be it.

I stopped patrolling during the afternoon and evening – I left that to the chaplains. It made me immensely sad to have to do this, but I had to protect myself from confrontation.

Were it not for the animosity I had encountered from some individuals, I'd probably still be patrolling today. But fate dealt me another card. I'd saved a woman and been lambasted for it – it was the final straw.

I also decided it was time to close down the charity. I called an Extraordinary General Meeting and explained to the trustees that I felt it was time to wrap things up. I was immensely sad, but I knew I couldn't go on like this. Closing the charity made me feel that I was closing off the memory of Maggie, but several people pointed out that her name would always live on – and that her name had raised a lot of money and increased awareness of Beachy Head and its problems. I hadn't managed to achieve 24-hour cover, but I'd saved many lives, I'd raised lots of money; put simply, I'd done all that I could. I'd worked hard and now it was all coming to an end. It was something I had no choice but to accept.

I made a statement to the press to explain that I was cutting back on my patrols and closing the charity. Afterwards, Val and I flew off to Spain. We both needed a break and wanted to avoid the barrage of phone calls that would inevitably follow my statement.

The phone calls came, but I ignored most of the requests for interviews. However, when I received a message from *Tonight With Trevor McDonald*, I was intrigued. A recent news item at the time had highlighted the case of two police community support officers (PCSOs) who had been present when a boy had drowned, but had been powerless to save him. In light of this, Trevor McDonald and his team were making a programme about whether or not Health and Safety laws were actually leading to the deaths of innocent people. My battle up at Beachy Head had been reported in the press, so they wanted me to go on the show to discuss how the laws had impacted upon me and to hear my opinion.

I felt honoured to be asked on the show and agreed to fly back from Spain for the interview. It was a wild 24 hours. I flew back at night, met the McDonald film crew at 7 am the following morning, did the interviews and was back on a plane by mid-afternoon! I was asked if I thought Health and Safety laws were too heavy handed, and – as you can probably guess – my reply was a resolute 'Yes!'

It's a sad state of affairs – one human being is prevented from helping another because of the law that says they need appropriate training or a rope tied around their waist.

CHAPTER 21

WITH MY HEAD HELD HIGH

My last ever incident was one of the simplest. It was October 2007, and I was only patrolling in the mornings. One day I spotted a girl in a hooded top, and as soon as she spotted me she started running. She was about 18 and fit and I was nearly 57. I knew I didn't have a hope of catching her, but could see that she was heading towards Shooters Hill, so I decided to run back to my car and drive in the hope I could head her off.

I ran up Shooters Hill and, sure enough, she was hurtling towards me.

'Stop right there!' I shouted. 'What are you doing? Is there a problem?'

She was blonde and pretty and it turned out she had problems at college. She couldn't cope with life and was fed up with people telling her to pull herself together because, quite simply, she couldn't. It was a simple case to solve. We talked, I advised her to seek help, and she agreed. In many ways, it was the most unremarkable of incidents, but at the same time it was of huge significance to me.

As I watched her drive off, I reflected on my age. I hadn't been able to chase the girl on foot and I couldn't help but think how terrible it would have been if she had gone over the edge before I'd got to her. I'd been lucky – she'd had plenty of time to jump before I got to her – and if I'd lost her it would have destroyed me emotionally. If I keep patrolling, I thought, I'm only going to set myself up for disaster one day. I'd had my fair share of tragedy and I began to feel that my time was up – I didn't want to be vulnerable to tragedy any more. I also wondered if I was getting too old for patrolling.

For the past three-and-a-half years, I'd been getting up at 4.30 am every day, seven days a week, whatever the weather. I was always up at the Head by 5.30 am, even if it was minus five degrees, or pouring with rain in the pitch black of winter. I'd patrolled in thick fog, in gale-force winds and I'd walked the six-and-half-mile stretch religiously; it was only now that I realised I was beginning to get bored. I wasn't bored of saving lives; I was bored of the conflict with those who didn't want me up there. I never expected anyone to thank me for my work, but now that I was being attacked and bad-mouthed I could not help but feel down about what I was doing. I drove home filled with doubt. I would continue patrolling for a while, but somehow my heart was no longer in it.

The moment I decided to quit completely came during an interview. I was up at the edge with a team from Meridian TV. The interview was about the conflicts I'd experienced and the Health and Safety issues I had come up against. I talked about my problems with the coastguards and some chaplains, and explained why I had cut my patrols back to mornings only. The interviewer asked me what I was planning on doing next. He wanted to know how I was planning to proceed in the face of such difficulties, but even I was surprised by my answer.

'I can walk away from this with my head held high,' I told him. The words came about before I had a chance to think. As I heard myself saying them I realised that now was my moment. I was right. I *could* walk away with my head held high. The time had come for me to do just that. That's it, I thought, I'm going to pack it all up.

'So you're not going to patrol any more?' asked the journalist. From the look on his face, I could tell he hadn't expected the interview to take such a turn.

'No,' I replied. 'This is it.'

I explained I had finally had enough. I was tired, the pressure was too much and the conflicts were too bitter. I was ready to step away from the edge for good. The interview finished and I let out a deep breath. I'd had an epiphany. It was all over.

I walked back to my car feeling good. Three years, I thought, as I shut the door. Never again would I shut the door after a patrol. I started the car and pulled away. As I drove past Beachy Head, I gazed across the landscape that had been a part of me for such a long time. I thought of all the time I'd spent on those hills, and I felt proud of what I had achieved. At the same time, it was as if a massive weight had been lifted from my shoulders. I'd come to the end of my journey.

★   ★   ★

I walked through the front door with a massive grin on my face.

'What's the matter with you?' said Val as she kissed me. 'Are you all right?'

It must have been a while since she'd seen me beam like that.

'I'm fine,' I said. 'I've just made a big decision. I've finished. I'm never going back.'

'*Really*?' she replied, wide eyed.

'It's over,' I said. 'It's really over.'

Val gave me an enormous hug and I felt a huge sense of release. She had been right when she'd told me only I would know when I was ready to stop. I felt the pressure and tension drain from me. Suddenly, I felt I was ready to live normally again. It was time to move on and I felt great.

That night, I went to bed without setting my alarm, yet I still woke up on the dot at 4.30 am. I was halfway out of bed before I remembered my decision. No Keith, I thought, you don't have to go in today. I had a little chuckle to myself and slipped back into the warmth of the bed. I cuddled up to Val and drifted back into a delicious sleep.

*   *   *

What a journey I've been on, I thought to myself in the days after I decided to walk away from the edge for good. It was only once I stopped patrolling that I really had time to reflect on how my life had changed since meeting Maggie. My mind boggled when I looked back – so much had happened that it was staggering. I'd loved, lost and now I'd found love again and it amazed me. I'd been from the dizzy heights of joy to the depths of despair and now I was in a different place altogether. I was happy and strong again. I had found peace.

I saved many people up at Beachy Head – more than I could mention in this book – but at the same time they saved me and nurtured me through the grieving process. I have learned so much from those I have spoken to. I have learned to listen, to advise, and I've learned to put my own problems in perspective. I've become able to talk about the pain of losing my wife to suicide and at the same time I have come to terms with losing a loved one. I can talk about Maggie freely now – the mention of her name doesn't break my heart any more. Rather, it gives me fond memories of a woman who, during her life and through her death, made me the man I am today. Not that I have cast Maggie from my mind completely – you cannot fall in love and then forget about someone. There will always be a place in my heart for her, but it is a happy place rather than a sad one.

I'm away from the edge now, but Maggie's cross remains. I visit occasionally so that I can pay my respects, clean it and re-varnish it. I only hope that now I'm no longer there to offer my help, seeing this symbol of Maggie's life and death may lead some people to think twice about jumping. I visit at Christmas and I will never forget to drive to Beachy Head on 2 March, the anniversary of the day Maggie died. But I no longer visit on our anniversary. I have a new life with Val, and a new anniversary to celebrate with a woman who is very much alive and deeply precious to me.

Fate led me to Beachy Head and fate led me away from it. The time came to stop, but that moment coincided with Val needing me to be there for her more and more. Her Parkinson's means that I will need to be free to devote myself to her 100 per cent in the future, but for the time being we are making the most of every moment we have together. In March this year, Val underwent heart surgery and came through it with her characteristic strength of mind and vitality. The recovery process is a long and painful one, but it hasn't stopped us loving and laughing with each other and our friends. We're planning another trip around the world, we're planning to get back on the ski slopes as soon as the doctor gives Val the OK, yet we're also very focused living life in the moment, living life for today.

The future is never certain, and tomorrow doesn't always come. As I finish writing about my journey, I know that another one awaits me. And I am ready for it. At the moment, I feel blessed every morning I wake up with Val by my side. It's all I could ask for after those rollercoaster years living life on the edge.